CHINA INSIDE OUT

CHINESE INNOVATORS IN THEIR OWN WORDS

BASED ON THE BEIWANGLU PODCAST

BY BESSIE LEE

WRITTEN BY PETER BOMER

PREFACE

THE BEIWANGLU PODCAST

This is the first in a series of publications based on Beiwanglu (贝望录), an award-winning weekly Chinese Podcast.

Beiwanglu features conversations between real businesspeople and leading Chinese entrepreneurs, investors and innovators. Our aim is to offer informal, straightforward, 'peer to peer' insight into what really goes on at the grass roots of modern Chinese commerce.

Beiwanglu appeared on Apple's prestigious 'Best Podcast' and 'Most Popular New Podcast' lists in its launch year (2019) and now has over 250,000 subscribers.

As you might expect, the podcast offers considerable wit, wisdom and insight, but, sadly, only to those who are fluent in Chinese. The China Inside Out series aims to make these insights available to non-Chinese speakers, whether they be actively engaged with China or merely China-curious.

CONTRIBUTORS

Chienling Bessie Lee (李倩玲)

Beiwanglu was conceived by lead host, Bessie Lee, Founder and CEO of Withinlink, a China-based start-up incubator and early- stage venture fund focused on Chinese digital & marketing technology.

Bessie is well-known in the Chinese media, marketing & communications industry. Her 30-year career spans roles as CEO at Mindshare, Greater China CEO at WPP PLC and recently, more unusual C-level roles across industries. She has been an active player in the development of Chinese digital marketing from inception to its current position as a world leader, boasting the largest, most engaged population of mobile internet users on the planet.

Bessie co-founded the Mobile Marketing Association in China, is a popular blogger, frequent media commentator, sought-after international speaker, and holder of numerous prestigious international and domestic awards.

Jennie Liu (刘雨静)

Bessie's co-host is Jennie Liu, a senior journalist at Shanghai Press Group's financial and business news platform, Jiemian News. She covers international and local company news with a focus on consumer marketing.

She won a Silver Award in 2018 and a Bronze Award in 2019 respectively for best business creative content at the ROI Festival, the largest creative award in the Greater China region, and was also named 'Outstanding Journalist' by Jiemian News in 2019.

She holds a master's degree in communication management from the USC Annenberg School for Communication and Journalism.

PREFACE

Peter Bomer (马乐天)

Peter is a serial entrepreneur, business advisor, investor, writer and China hand. He first visited Taiwan in 1998, quickly became a regular business traveller to the mainland and moved to Shanghai soon after as part of the leadership team tasked with re-launching Diageo Plc in China.

In 2007, he launched his first Chinese start-up (a Chinese-language radio broadcaster, covering 14 provinces and regularly achieving industry-best audience profile & ratings). He has since launched a string of businesses in China, as well as assisting many overseas brands into the market. Peter is editor and chief writer for the China Inside Out series.

THE INTERVIEWEES

Wang Zhimin (王智民) is Founder & Chairman of Nova Vision, a leading Chinese ophthalmic company and pioneering multi-Channel business.

Hou Yongpu (侯永璞) is Founder of Yongpu Coffee, the highest selling liquid coffee brand on Tmall, having achieved annual sales of more than RMB 400 million within 4 years of launch.

Wu Xiaobo (吴晓波) is a best-selling Chinese business writer, economist, investor and entrepreneur. He is visiting scholar at Harvard University & former professor of EMBA courses at Shanghai Jiao Tong and Jinan Universities.

Liu Xiaolu (刘小璐) co-founded NEIWAI, a pioneering Chinese underwear brand, in 2012. NEIWAI now has over one million repeat customers, 2.2 million social media followers, and distributes both on & offline.

Ms Liu was featured in Fortune China's "Future List of China's Most Influential Businesswomen." In 2021.

Chen Yaping (陈雅萍) has over thirty years of experience in brand marketing, advertising, media where she was and e-commerce operations, most recently as marketing director at Myk +, a Danish brand offering ethical cleaning and care products for mother and baby, responsible for market entry & subsequent growth.

NOTE ON TEXT

Our guests, the podcast team and authors all have many years of China business experience to draw upon and we hope you will find our combined ideas, insights, opinions and observations insightful and useful.

That said, we acknowledge that all content here represents our combined subjective opinion, not hard fact, and may be open to different interpretation or disagreement.

We would be grateful to hear of any factual errors so that we can amend in future editions. Any such mistakes are of course solely those of the authors and not of our team or guests.

NOTE ON TRANSLATION

The podcast transcripts featured here were translated from the Chinese by local agencies in Shanghai. Occasional quirks of wording and expression appear throughout, and these have been left unaltered in a spirit of authenticity.

PREFACE

ACKNOWLEDGMENTS

We'd like to express our gratitude to our guests, our listeners and especially to the Beiwanglu production team, who between them have carried out most of the actual hard work without which neither Beiwanglu, nor this book could exist.

For their positivity, effort and commitment, our heartfelt thanks to:
    Sweelynn Chong (*庄郭瑞玲*),
    'Helen' Zhao Haiwen (赵海文),
    'Stephy' Liu Qiongwei (刘琼蔚), before 2022,
    & 'Vivian' Cao Ningning (曹宁宁), thereafter.

———

FOREWORD

WHY WE WROTE THIS BOOK

Our small editorial team is a mix of western & Chinese with a combined total of more than 90 years spent living and working in mainland China.

As we produced the podcasts and compared them to our own experience, we began to see that they offer unusual insight into the Chinese business mind. This is explicit in the observations and opinions expressed by our guests of course, but it's the attitudes and assumptions they reveal inadvertently, through the informal, conversational format of a podcast, which are sometimes most illuminating.

As the body of episodes grew many themes recurred and stimulated a good deal of debate. Ultimately, we came to see that despite our different backgrounds, we had all reached broadly similar conclusions as to why it is so difficult for foreign businesses to succeed here.

ALIEN NATIONS

At root, the issue is cultural and it's a thorny one, boiling down to a tension between two forces in Chinese life:

First, people are people; the Chinese, like everyone, possess the full range of personality types, abilities, aspirations, anxieties and emotions: the need for love, companionship, friendship & family, the desire for security and success.

Second, where we in the West value progress, the Chinese value continuity and a return to what they regard as the natural order 'under heaven'.

This is partly a function of the pride and sense of self-worth inspired by 3000 years or more of recorded history & cultural continuity. It also has much to do with the differently structured minds formed by a language which is immensely expressive, yet fixed and relatively unchanging. The Chinese believe that they have a word for every concept under heaven. If an idea isn't already described in Chinese, it follows for many that it can't be important and may not even be real.

MISCONCEPTION, MISUNDERSTANDING & DISSONANCE

Westerners are usually fairly accepting of this as reasonable in theory, yet often struggle to accept the vastness of the gulf between Chinese & western ideas when confronted by it in practice.

Our shared humanity means that for westerners living and working there, much of everyday life in China feels normal and familiar. Moments of mutual incomprehension are the exception, but their rarity serves to amplify the cultural shock and disorientation they cause.

Scholars, travellers & assorted western experts have built a considerable body of work aimed at explaining the differences. Inevitably, their theories are coloured by their own cultural perspective and the result can be simplistic; sometimes plain wrong.

For example, it's common to hear generalisations about the collective nature of Chinese society. This, contrasted with western 'individualism', offers a neat explanation for our divergent worldviews; one which fits our western sense of what is reasonable. But as any long-term visitor to China will understand, it does a severe disservice to the Chinese, who, by a wide margin, are more irrepressibly individualist than most in the West.

The concept of 'Guanxi' is another frequently misunderstood phenomenon, usually taken to mean that to get on in China one must entertain, host dinners and generally invest in building personal relationships.

It doesn't hurt of course; but it isn't Guanxi, which refers to the networks of individuals, rooted in extended family, early acquaintance and life-long- association, which once offered the only reliable source of mutual support in a historically uncertain China.

Devastation by flood, famine, disease or general upheaval was commonplace until fairly modern times. The ability to depend absolutely upon a tight-knit network was a necessity, if sometimes still insufficient for survival. By definition, these networks excluded outsiders.

Life in modern China is vastly more benign and predictable for most people, but Guanxi culture remains deeply rooted. The idea that affability and generosity, however sincere and expansive, could grant an outsider trusted membership of the inner networks is misguided.

WHY HIGHLIGHT THESE MISCONCEPTIONS?

Reflecting on my own early China experience, I was often confounded by the way in which Chinese people behaved just as we do in everyday settings: children's mannerisms and play, social interaction, the obvious affection between old married couples; all expressed in ways that were perfectly familiar. And yet, in responding to events, especially in business, Chinese actions often seemed utterly inexplicable.

Few western businesses have achieved substantive, long-term success in China. Those that have, invested for the very long-term and were prepared to take their knocks, often severe. Failure is the norm and often stems from an unwillingness to accept that our differences could truly be as profound as they seem. The view (now happily discredited) that with modernity, Chinese minds & customs would change to resemble our own has also played a part. They haven't yet and won't.

The Chinese entrepreneurs featured in these conversations are impressive on their own terms. They are busy creating China's commercial future by finding novel twists on traditional approaches to business. Increasingly, they and their like will be the partners, customers and competitors for any international business operating in China.

Bearing all of this in mind then, the aim of this book is to showcase the expertise and achievements of the interviewees so as to offer practical insights into the nature of Chinese business practice and opportunity.

Perhaps most of all, we hope to call readers' attention to

the many small tells and nuances within these conversations which illustrate the Chinese worldview and business mindset, its strengths and limitations.

People are people and business is business, but Chinese culture *is* inherently different, alien even, to the western mind. It's no exaggeration to say that after nearly 20 years in China, the author has observed hundreds of otherwise rational, intelligent and able westerners who simply refuse to accept this.

1
DIGITAL TRANSFORMATION IN CHINESE RETAIL

We start with an insight into the workings of China's emerging consumer markets, the technology which enables them and the general business environment in recent years.

Wang Zhimin, our guest, is widely known and respected in China. He is an unusual character, exemplifying many of the most intriguing traits of Chinese entrepreneurs but with a sophistication of vision which sets him apart.

Mr Wang gives an excellent overview of the sheer scale of the Chinese market; in reality, a set of related, but sometimes quite varied regional markets, and illuminates the extreme pace of change which to the Chinese seems normal but which is often bewildering to international entrants.

In doing this, he illustrates many of China's accepted modes of business thought and practice, the limited horizons in which planning takes place and how, though still rarely, this is all being challenged by the very practical creativity of leading entrepreneurs.

We also see highlighted one of China's key differences: the 'accidental uniqueness' of its digital and media environment.

Editor's note: To understand what we mean by this, click to view the New York Times' YouTube video 'How China is Changing Your Internet', or scan the QR code below. The video is quite old now and some of the specifics have changed but it's entertaining and still the best summary we know of China's digital eco-system & the sometimes unintentionally benign consequences of the 'Great Firewall'.

For the most part, our commentaries take the view that the differences between China and the West are vaster and more strange than is easily appreciated and that many failures to engage productively arise from this. It's worth noting therefore that not everything is different; that China still shares certain characteristics with us.

I'm thinking in particular of the short-term nature of planning and decision making; standard practice in China and, if for slightly different reasons, still the norm in large organisations worldwide. That China's characteristics sometimes coincide with ours shouldn't come as a surprise;

Chinese culture and history *are* profound and bemusing influences for sure, but, as we've already highlighted, basic human motivations are similar the world over.

In China, a short-term, transactional mindset is deeply engrained; the product of survival instincts finely honed over centuries of routine exposure to life or death events.

Why would anyone who lived through the 1960's & 70's have worked towards cultivating future profits when they had no especially strong expectation of being around to reap the benefits?

Why would any 90's tech start-up from Shenzhen, arising out of poverty and lacking exposure to 'mature international business practice', think beyond the entrepreneurial approach that gave it its impressive early growth?

Editor's note: for further insight into China's innately entrepreneurial mindset see chapter three, featuring Wu Xiaobo, the distinguished business author and serially successful entrepreneur.

This brings us to a topic which will be a major theme in future publications: an approach to innovation which recalls "moving fast and breaking things" but might better be described as "moving fast and breaking nothing if you can help it" (in China, it seems, you usually can). It's an area of real excellence for the Chinese; one in which we think they have much to teach the rest of the world.

The approach (we call it 'Scruffy Innovation') has more to do with rapid testing of multiple variations in form and approach than it is with creativity or deep thought. Ideas are put into practice quickly, often while only half formed.

These are developed 'live', in-market, subject to a high degree of senior managerial awareness and savvy which allows them to be rapidly tweaked and teased into shape, or equally quickly discontinued, with any negative fallout managed away.

It's a constant process of trial and error and relies on the Chinese genius for establishing what works at extraordinary speed so as to either double-down or desist. A fundamentally practical approach, it requires direct control from the top and is governed by a hard-bitten awareness of short-term financial impact above all else.

You might recognise a similarity to Eric Ries' 'Lean Start-up' approach, but in China, this is more instinctual, intuitive and dynamic. It rejects the idea of learning though trial and error (mistakes may be costly) in favour of adapting at a pace which allows for profitability from the outset. Experience suggests that the Chinese are uniquely good at it.

It's still the case that senior leadership in many of the Shenzhen tech giants continues to take a highly entrepreneurial approach; unstructured, fast moving, selectively micro-managing and dominated by a small inner circle if not a single charismatic figure. Where the elder statesmen and women of modern Chinese business have led, so younger entrepreneurs have followed.

Scruffy Innovation has its disadvantages. Top teams may move fast, but lower levels of management who aren't directly involved in any given initiative are often unaware. We know a number of cases in which unsuspecting teams found themselves in direct competition with their own colleagues in other departments. The transactional mindset is a problem too, prioritising short term profit over long term sustainability.

Perhaps the real lesson from Wang Zhimin and Baodao Optical is that when an inspirational leader succeeds in marrying depth of thought and a long-term perspective to their innate Scruffy Innovative abilities, the results can be extraordinary.

Editor's note: readers may be aware that China's digital landscape is very different to that in the West. For a solid general overview, covering many of the platforms discussed in this dialogue, try 'The Shift in China's Digital landscape' published by Digital Crew, or scan the QR code below:

Transcript
Digital Transformation Traditional Opticals
Broadcast on November 18, 2020
Hosted by Bessie Lee

Guest
Wang Zhimin (王智民)

. . .

Founder of Nova Vision, one of the first true multi-channel businesses in China. The company is a globally recognised leader in ophthalmic research & development with a market leading portfolio of brands including Baodao and MILANNO.

Mr Wang holds the prestigious Tianjin University award for 'Outstanding Contribution to the Integration of Engineering and Science' and is an honorary academician of the SAP China Research Institute, a visiting professor at Tainjin University's Ophthalmology School, and a Deputy Director and Expert Committee Member of the Enterprise Information Strategy and Innovation Research Centre at Guanghua School of Management, Beijing University.

With more than 600 million near-sighted people in China, prescription glasses are a necessity for many.

The optical industry is still a relatively fragmented market. Besides eyewear chain brands such as Baodao Optical, we have also seen various small optical stores competing on low-price strategies. With the traditional eyewear retail industry challenged by e-commerce, how to balance social e-commerce, online retail and optometry in the physical stores is something that many companies face.

In this episode of Beiwanglu, we invited Wang Zhimin, Chairman of Nova Vision, to talk about the current status of China's optical industry, the digital transformation attempts of Baodao Optical and the opportunities and challenges they encountered in their digital transformation.

Bessie

Today, we have Wang Zhimin, Chairman of Baodao

Optical Group, to talk to us about the digital transformation of enterprises.

How many years has Baodao Optical been operating in Mainland China, and what is the current business scale?

Wang Zhimin

We started our business in Mainland China in 1997. That year, we opened stores in Wuhan, Tianjin, Xiamen, and Fuzhou.

This first phase from 1997 to 2001 was considered a trial. One day in 2001, the front page of Xiamen Daily announced that China's GDP per capita had officially exceeded 1,000 USD, which is equivalent to 10,000 USD today. It was a huge opportunity for the market. Companies founded in that era would have grown considerably by now if they kept focusing on their own business. Standing on the shoulders of giants, how could it not succeed?

The second phase began when I officially took over the company in 2010. I felt that our brand name Baodao Optical would limit our future development. So we built the Nova Vision Group on top of Baodao Optical. Nova Vision, as the parent company, is a more professional business focusing on vision care. Because it is a more 2B (to business) oriented brand, most people are more familiar with Baodao Optical.

The third phase is e-commerce operations. In 2013, we started engaging with our customers and competing on various e-commerce platforms. For many start-up companies, we are already a senior e-commerce player.

The fourth phase is all about the changes and transformation that started in 2015.

. . .

Bessie

I've known you for years. And I know you started your company's digital transformation about five years ago, with many business-level changes across the back end, middle platform, and front end. Your recent big move of operating as an MCN (multi-channel network) with over 2,000 employees across the company drew a lot of attention. This is an interesting innovation in this industry. How did this concept emerge, and how exactly does it work?

Wang Zhimin

Our e-commerce department was established in 2010. Between 2010 and 2012, we had two e-commerce departments located in Beijing and Shanghai. They were primarily doing test projects until 2012 when we merged them into a strategic level department at our headquarters.

From 2012 to 2014, we witnessed the rise of Tmall (a Chinese B2C online retail website, spun off from Taobao, operated by the Alibaba Group) and the fierce competition among evolving group-buying websites.

Since then, I have been trying to figure out how we will face a new era. I've spent a lot of time talking to people from the internet industry and engaging with various sourcing platforms. We had a partnership with Dianping (a popular online directory for discovering local businesses, similar to Yelp) long before they merged.

After two years, I gradually understood the logic of platform e-commerce. The key is to accumulate a large enough user base and then distribute the traffic generated by these users for profit. This business logic is similar to the shopping malls, which create various activities to entice consumers to their malls, generating the traffic needed to attract businesses to open stores in the malls and pay rent. It is essentially the same idea, and it is the future.

We completed our entire digitisation process around 2019. Between 2017 and 2019, we tried various popular platforms at the time, from WeChat micro-business at the beginning, later known as social e-commerce, and then membership e-commerce. We sought professional help for each platform we entered. There were many third-party consulting companies dedicated to serving those who wished to enter these big platforms. We can call them MCN or training companies.

For example, there are plenty of so-called operation companies on Douyin (a video-sharing focused social networking service owned by Chinese company Byte-Dance). You can contract with them, and they will be responsible for making your account popular, or if you have plans to do a large operation on Douyin, they can send professionals over to assist you. In the beginning, we hired some professionals to teach us how to do marketing on WeChat. One of the most important concepts is to build a personal IP and public image.

Building a public image involves the careful design of articles and posts on various platforms. And establishing a personal IP basically means monetising an individual's IP traffic, which requires following a certain methodology.

Last year, we collaborated with Mao Buyi (a Chinese singer) for a campaign, and the results were good.

However, I have a question that has never been answered. A campaign that used 50% of our budget for the whole year, with over 10 million RMB in expenses, what resources did it bring us in the end? The fans brought in by

Mao Buyi only created a good short-term buzz for us. Putting aside the sales generated by the campaign, some of our important KPIs and expectations were not met.

I've been working on the concept of a user-end closed-loop business, where each employee becomes a user-end closed-loop business in the WeChat ecosystem. An employee can achieve this goal if they operate their WeChat account properly.

Our 20-30 million RMB yearly advertising budget is not big enough for us to find a competent advertising agency, let alone hire a 4A advertising agency. 300,000 RMB per month in advertising expenses is typical for a company like ours, but the benefits of a 300,000 RMB advertising plan seem insignificant. When foreign brands start to realise this problem, 4A advertising agencies will be in big trouble.

When we saw the possibility of the user-end closed-loop business in WeChat, we decided to stop our careless advertising spending. With our $20 million advertising budget, I believe our employees would be delighted and committed to marketing even if only half of the budget were given to them.

I have a friend who owns a restaurant business, and he is always participating in events and posting reviews on Dianping to improve his account level

Editor's note: Dianping user accounts are ranked, with higher level accounts having greater visibility. Try this concise overview by Hi Com or scan the QR code below:

He thinks that Dianping has a great influence on the success of a restaurant business. Companies that sell goods depend on Tmall, while restaurants depend on Dianping.

We generally didn't understand the nature of the platform and the best practices for operating on it. The only thing we knew was that sending out coupons on the platform would bring traffic. Our actions were all results-driven, and we only paid for campaigns that might generate traffic.

After two weeks of continuous use of Dianping, I started my experiment. I called a colleague from the marketing department and asked him to manage our operations in Dianping. He didn't have any experience of doing operations on Dianping. I showed him everything he needed to do to level up his user rank.

After reaching level eight, any posts by his account will have a much higher visibility on Dianping. And our goal was to mobilise all 8,000 employees in our company to become active users of Dianping. Of the 700 to 800 people in our Shanghai headquarters, only two had a high user level (seven and eight), while the rest had a user level below three.

This meant that there was a great potential for us to improve our ranking. We started by creating a discussion group for the several hundred employees in our Shanghai headquarters and introduced some guidelines on using Dianping.

We asked everyone to do daily check-ins at Dianping and offered a reward of 100 RMB per person per day. By the fifth day, we had mobilised over 2,000 employees to join, and two months later, everyone in our company had joined the campaign. Everyone was willing to write content on Dianping, of course, with some incentives. We calculated that it only cost us 160,000 RMB to get 8,000 active users on Dianping.

Bessie

I thought you spent a lot of money on this.

Wang Zhimin

A single campaign with Mao Buyi cost us more than 10 million RMB. And it only cost me 160,000 RMB to turn all our employees into active Dianping users, which enabled us to do a lot of operations in the future. After about six months of operation on Dianping, we expanded to another important platform, RED (one of China's most popular social shopping platforms).

We also invited professionals to give us training on operations on RED, and so far, we have turned some 800 employees into active RED users. As we learned more about the platform, we realised that all the platforms have similar operating logic with minor differences. For example, Dianping has no requirements for user-generated content, but if a user doesn't post according to guidelines on RED, they won't be able to get traffic.

So this is how the idea of using employees as MCNs came to be. Our most important move in 2020 was to change our entire human resource model. We encourage all our colleagues to operate their own IP well, and I will start giving out more financial incentives to encourage content creation and operation on different platforms. This is of great value to them and our company.

Bessie

What is the significance to Baodao Optical and your employees in getting them to become active users of Dianping and encouraging them to upgrade their user level?

Wang Zhimin

We have five goals: finding public domain traffic, generating more buzz, creating needs, forming a user-end closed-loop business, and doing membership operations.

We consider Dianping as a public domain traffic platform to attract potential customers and develop a customer relationship. It doesn't matter if our employees have reached certain user levels on Dianping. The important thing is that they have acquired the necessary marketing skills in the process.

Bessie

With all this effort, Baodao Optical should now top the search result relating to eyewear on the Dianping. Right?

Wang Zhimin

That's true, but it's a shame that we didn't manage our Dianping account properly in the beginning. Our partnership with Dianping started in 2013. For the first seven to eight years, our official account was unattended, and we didn't have anyone to respond to consumer complaints. We should have promptly attended to our customers' complaints on such an important public domain traffic platform. A consumer willing to complain still has at least a little faith in the brand. If they don't bother to complain, they must be extremely disappointed, and we will lose this consumer forever.

Bessie

Your company's digital transformation began around 2010. Besides your well-known success story of running your employees as an MCN, do you have any other successful digital case studies for us?

Wang Zhimin

The highlight of this year is not our MCN efforts. Before November, most of the people who came to speak to us were more interested in private domain traffic. We had a major restructuring of our business in 2015, which began with our exploration into the outlook of Eyewear 3.0.

China's optical industry has been lagging behind, and the public has little understanding of the industry. For example, the average time spent on eye tests in Chinese optical stores is about five minutes. Sometimes it's the same case in hospitals. The optometry process takes about 45 minutes to one hour in the US, UK, and Australia.

· · ·

Bessie

That's a big difference.

Wang Zhimin

Why does the optometry process that takes an hour in the US only take 5 minutes in China? The optometry process in the US is not just an eyewear fitting test but a comprehensive vision examination. They check for eye diseases, strabismus and amblyopia, vision differences between day and night, and so on.

If authorities do not focus on public vision health and allocate more resources to promote vision care, consumers will not pay more attention to vision health. Everyone will treat fitting glasses like buying a piece of new clothing. The essence of the optical industry is healthcare, which many people have not seen clearly.

In 2011, we introduced a professional optometrist training program similar to those in Australia, the UK, and the US. We spent ten years training the largest group of optometrists in China, with a total of 1600 people. Starting in 2015, in our exploration of Eyewear 3.0, we have made our optometrists the centre of interaction with consumers, and the whole service process revolves around them. Our digitisation is based on the interaction between optometrists and consumers.

Another important digital infrastructure is E-learning, which we started very early. All our training is recorded. If we can train 40 people in one session, why not train 8,000 people? Now all of our training courses are available on video, and 98% of the digital training material in the entire optical industry are ours. Although there are lots of training in the industry, few have been systematically digitalised.

Bessie

Is all your training online now?

Wang Zhimin

Yes, it is all online. Our training is not all about optometry but also includes users' community operation and building IP and public image. Our online training is available every day.

Bessie

I don't think you're too worried about your employees being recruited by other companies, right? Because you can use online training to get new employees up and running quickly.

Wang Zhimin

No, it's still a problem for us. Training staff is expensive. By making training more efficient, we can reduce some of the risks. When we have a large number of employees, creating a platform that is fun for them can also help reduce staff turnover, which is a bonus in this case. As for how to regulate the behaviour of employees on social media, I don't think we need to worry about it. Because each platform has its own rules, users who are out of line will be blocked and will not have a significant impact. As for the users with different personalities and preferences, each platform will also handle them with labelling and classification.

For example, our social media users are divided into two types: those who focus on fashion and those who position themselves as professionals, i.e., ophthalmologists. Doctors like to answer questions and share knowledge as professionals on Zhihu (a knowledge sharing website where questions are created, answered, edited and organised by the community of its users), where they display their expertise, and hearsay can be easily debunked by other professionals. The fashion-oriented group finds Zhihu boring.

Different platforms have a unique appeal to various personality groups. Such innovation is driven so easily in our company because it responds to human nature. In contrast, rules that prohibit employees from using cell phones during work are purely against human nature in many retail companies. We encourage employees to use all kinds of social media and to use them well.

Bessie

You are personally engaged in the whole process of your company's digital transformation. And I know many other companies would create a position like a chief innovation officer to lead such transformation. I also heard that you once created a similar position but then eliminated it. Why?

Wang Zhimin

Before the MCN reform, we had a one to two million RMB fund every year to reward employees who made special contributions in innovation. But very rarely have we ever given out more than 30% of this fund as bonus. Employees initially tried very hard to submit ideas, but many of them were not feasible. The issue is that the proposals need to be submitted, discussed in meetings, and reviewed by the boss. By the time the proposal is approved, it might be half a year later. The idea may have lost its feasibility.

This formal approach does not work. It is also mindless to give out money without a review process. This problem was completely solved after turning all our employees into active users on the major social media platforms. The hardest part of innovation is setting KPIs and designing the closed loop. But it's easy to set KPIs by putting quantitative criteria on these platforms. For example, the account rankings are indicators that could be evaluated.

Bessie

Because it's your own company, you're willing to put so much effort into doing everything hands-on. For a professional CEO hired by a company, I guess their sense of urgency to transform the company would be very different.

Wang Zhimin

Yes, particularly in a foreign enterprise in China. Milan Jiang (an advertising professional with more than 20 years of experience in retail and mobile marketing in China) believes this is a coherent methodology after reviewing our entire transformation process.

If a company follows this approach and continues to iterate on specific practices, it will become more and more competitive. But Milan Jiang feels that her clients are not ready to do such hard work. In practice, it's too painful for either the marketing or the sales department to drive such a transformation. But we have at least accomplished this transformation and proved to everyone that it is a viable path to digital transformation for companies.

Bessie

Your company must have encountered a lot of 'pitfalls' in the transformation process. Can you share with us the areas we should pay special attention to?

Wang Zhimin

There are a lot of 'pitfalls', most of them are hidden in the process of digitalisation.

The high risk of digitalisation is due to how fast technology evolves, and if you fail to choose the right direction, it may cause significant losses. We bought a complex CRM system before, and now it's a huge depreciation expense on the company's books.

The other hidden problem is having a great vision, but insufficient team execution capacity or having a leader with biased perceptions.

We generally judge the probability of a company's transformation success in three aspects: the leader's level of awareness, the team's ability, and the capability to execute plans. The worst combination could be a leader with limited recognition who picks the wrong direction. A team with excellent execution moves forward in a series of bad choices, and the company ends up in trouble very quickly.

. . .

Jennie

Wang Zhimin mentioned that the nature of the optical industry is vision care. However, my observation is that the domestic optical industry is more like a fragmented retail business with low concentration. How did Baodao Optical achieve its current scale in such a market? And you mentioned the gap between the domestic optical industry and overseas markets. Will our domestic industry move towards more specialised optometry and vision care in the future?

Wang Zhimin

This problem is common in the retail industry in China. The chain management of many domestic companies can be more professional, efficient, and centralised.

For example, there are probably hundreds of thousands of pet stores in China, but rarely is there a chain. There are nearly 500,000 pharmacies in China, and more than half of them are individual pharmacies, mainly because of the population density distribution in our country. Our market also has a lot of irregularities. For example, there are 1,080 directly managed Baodao optical stores but close to 4,000 knock off Baodao optical stores. We spent millions every year fighting against counterfeiting. The more we crack down, the more fake Baodao optical stores will appear. It is impossible to eliminate them completely. To operate a business and start-up properly, we need to be versatile in dealing with various risks and challenges.

I spoke with an executive at Mia (an online mother and baby product platform) about their transition from online to physical stores. They felt that the transformation was very challenging. And one thing that makes the Chinese market special is that online and offline converge with each other. The iteration of management practices is fast.

From management's perspective, Meituan's online operations are very efficient. (Meituan is an e-commerce platform providing life services in over 200 categories including food & beverage, food delivery, transport, travel and entertainment in over 2,800 counties and cities in China) Yet offline, they also have to manage a team of hundreds of thousands of people, which is a very impressive operational capability. However, from another perspective, e-commerce is so robust that it seems unnecessary to open more physical stores. Our goal in 2011 was to open 10,000 optical stores, but now this dream is impossible to accomplish. Because the efficiency of e-commerce is so high and the speed of technology so fast, it is no longer necessary to open 10,000 optical stores. Now my goal is to open 2,000 optical stores and apply the latest technology and methods to achieve the revenue of 10,000 stores. This is what we have been reflecting on at the moment.

Jennie

Baodao Optical has been working on digital transformation for a long time, but the whole optical industry still relies more on physical stores. In your opinion, how can a company in this industry achieve the revenue of 10,000 stores with 2,000 stores? What is the best approach to combining physical stores and e-commerce? Do you have any suggestions?

Wang Zhimin

The traditional optical industry has given up on our

kind of innovation strategy. One of the biggest challenges in operating a chain store is that you need to have the ability to manage different fields, including HR, platform, and technology. Our rivals are all lagging behind us in terms of scale.

Since 2015, we have invested at least 20 million RMB in IT and digitalisation every year, over 100 million RMB in five years. We firmly believe that digitalisation can deliver good outcomes. An important factor that makes digital transformation difficult is that it's hard to produce short-term results.

It is a phenomenon that traditional optical companies are becoming more localised. With the economic environment less optimistic now, they know it is impossible to take the countrywide chain path soon. So, they turn to developing the local market instead. A national chain does not necessarily mean a high level of competitiveness. Some locally rooted companies possess a high degree of competitiveness. That's why most of the traditional optical brands are cultivating the local market.

In the future, we will see many strong regional optical chains. There is also a new type of optical store that are started up by young people. They choose to open stores in office buildings instead of shopping malls, and they are skilled in using traffic and membership incentives to attract customers. They are good at utilising traffic but do not necessarily have strong expertise, which takes a long time to develop.

Bessie

Your strong desire to learn and act on digitisation is rare among the business owners I know. I often find you attending forums where you're not necessarily a speaker but rather a person who wants to learn new knowledge and concepts. You would also go around to visit major platforms in the early years and invite experts from various fields to your company to share their knowledge. I can feel your strong desire to learn.

Wang Zhimin

The future for Chinese business people is very daunting. You'll find all the classrooms in the universities in major cities full during weekends, where all the entrepreneurs or executives are studying. The spirit of learning is everywhere. The key is to find the right learning path.

The main challenge for traditional Chinese companies who want to transform is their decision-makers' limited understanding of technology. That's why I recently promoted a logic called digital thinking in our company. When our MOC (Member's Operation Centre) team held lectures in our company, some of our colleagues were confused because not everyone knows how to convert the traffic between WeChat mini app and WeChat official account inside their ecosystem, and where they might encounter problems.

I can tell you the types of forums our company usually participates in, such as fashion forums, e-commerce forums, AI forums, as we have AI deployed in our company, and medical forums and MCN forums.

Bessie

Are you deploying blockchain too?

. . .

Wang Zhimin

Two years ago, we were planning to link membership points with blockchain. The whole architecture is ready.

We are relatively competent and successful among the companies pushing digitalisation, but we still end up stepping into many 'pitfalls'. Sometimes the success of a new concept is not about whether the idea is good or bad. It's about doing the right thing at the right time.

Bessie

With all the experience and ideas you've accumulated over the years, things may not have worked out at the time, but you have formed a concept for it in your mind. When the opportunity matures after a few years, you can quickly find the concept, update it and put it into the market.

For many enterprises managed by a professional manager, if they want to invest ten million RMB in digitalisation every year like you, their bosses will definitely ask them, "What will this 10 million RMB bring?" There is no chance of trial and error, and there will be no technology and concept accumulation, and there will be no possibility for later yield.

Wang Zhimin

I strongly agree. Digitalisation will not be able to produce revenue quickly. When asked if they should spend 10 million RMB on digital transformation or hire Austin Li (a Chinese top beauty influencer, and the best live-streaming salesman of beauty products in China) to sell their products on his live-streaming platform with the same budget and generate 30 million RMB revenue, most bosses would choose Austin Li.

Bessie

Right, but the 30 million revenue is most likely a one-time deal. Austin Li might help you keep a relatively high exposure for about three to six months, but after which there will be no effect.

Wang Zhimin

That is why being the owner of a business is a very tiring job. You have to pay attention to various needs in the short, medium and long term at the same time. If you only look at sales and cash flow, you may not be able to cope with new changes in the market, such as a sudden change in consumer tastes, and you may lose a lot. Because you don't really own any users, how to maintain a relationship with the users and make the relationship sticky so that the users will really like your brand? This relationship takes a long time to create. This is the focus of the future.

Bessie

Today's show should be a source of inspiration for a lot of our young audience. We post a lot of content on social media, but we never think about how to build our own IP assets on these platforms. When you view it as an asset, you will feel totally different the next time you post content on WeChat or publish content on RED.

For enterprise managers, digital transformation is not easy, and it can be a very lonely road. I understand that when Wang Zhimin makes decisions, all 8,000 of his employees are counting on him, and he needs to decide what's best for the company. I have great respect for him as he has insisted on this path of digital transformation for so many years.

2
SCRUFFY INNOVATION AT YONGPU COFFEE

Our second selection may be most interesting for the way in which it highlights some of the common blind spots shared by businesses in China.

This in no way reflects badly on Chinese entrepreneurs, whose energy, passion and drive are often greater than those of their counterparts overseas. Instead, we believe that it reflects the relative youth of Chinese consumer markets and businesses, few of which have much history before 2010, most of which are accelerating along steep learning curves at a pace which ought to inspire envy and admiration in the West.

For example, there is a heavily product focused mindset on display here, and at times a lack of sophisticated consumer, product or market understanding.

The episode also contains plenty of conjecture expressed as hard fact in a tone which can verge on dogmatic. In fairness, this is partly a result of the challenge of translating Chinese into English, but at least in part it reflects a common mode of expression among Chinese entrepreneurs.

This 'mode' seems to reflect a process of self-education on behalf of the speaker; of crystallising lessons learned through experience in the speaker's mind by articulating them out loud. It may also owe something to the Chinese cultural reverence towards mastery of a skill and the desire to be acknowledged as possessing it.

So, while the episode is informative about who's doing what, it isn't necessarily as insightful about what makes the Chinese coffee market tick, or what will ultimately drive consumer preference and loyalty.

Why then, did we feel this episode was worthy of inclusion? Because we believe that it gives a great insight into the mind of the Chinese entrepreneur.

The attitude and approach on display here are common across many emerging Chinese industries and the businesses within them; businesses which will increasingly be the major competitors to new entrants from overseas. It's only by understanding these modes of thought that newcomers will be able to engage with them effectively. Given how few western businesses, large or small, have thrived in China, this is invaluable insight.

Our guest offers a good deal of theory in support of historic decisions made, not all of it convincing, some decidedly odd. This reflects the push for gaining understanding and perhaps a desire to believe that by stating forcefully that something is the case, it may become so.

In practice, these boldly stated theories often turn out to be quite elastic. They are continually adapted and updated to reflect the latest experience on the part of the speaker. To point out their 'fluidity' would be considered the height of bad manners and the ongoing shifts in perspective and opinion which one might hear from the same entrepreneur are rarely acknowledged by them or anyone else. This constant revisionism is actually healthy; it shows sensitivity towards the consequence of decisions made or actions carried out and leads to business playbooks which are ever more robust and credible with each evolution.

For better or worse, Yongpu coffee is a terrific case study in 'Scruffy Innovation'

> *Editor's note: see chapter one: the approach to business founded on rapid rollout of different formats and features, all with a view to quickly finding out what works and what doesn't at minimal financial loss.*

Many related characteristics can be inferred from the dialogue, such as a tendency to rapid instinctive calculation, often insightful, yet lacking much depth of analysis or understanding, or a general 'all things to all people' approach to brand positioning, in which a good product is one that's simultaneously smartly packaged, cheap, convenient, healthy *and* tasty.

In all of the above, one senses a desire for credibility and status, both for the individual and in pursuit of recognition for China as an equal in matters of business thought and practice. And why not? China may be a relative newcomer and still has much to explore and learn but they are doing it at a speed that no country in the western world could claim to have matched during their own industrial revolution.

One final thought: we think there's a lot in this episode that shows how very differently the Chinese perceive categories that we in the West take to be clearly defined, established and fixed. We are all prisoners of our cultural background and environment, and it doesn't always occur to us that the same rules just don't apply in China.

There are umpteen examples of this in the Chinese cultural sphere, applied both by western business *and* Chinese.

Ikea, for example, was widely viewed by locals as a super-premium, even luxury brand when it launched in China. There was much informal applause for this among western marketers in China at the time, given that Ikea enjoys more of a 'good value' (I hesitate to say 'cheap and cheerful') position in the West. Nevertheless, Ikea managed to maintain its enhanced reputation for several years, before the reality of traipsing through overcrowded and, by then, increasingly shabby showrooms undermined it. How was Ikea able to achieve this upmarket reputation at launch? because as a completely new proposition in the Chinese market, it was inherently exciting, different and thus special. This specialness was generally assumed and the Chinese had no point of comparison against which to benchmark the assumption.

Another noteworthy example is Matisse, a premium whisky from Taiwan, which launched in a curvy, cognac style bottle, with a French brand name. This would be almost inconceivable in the west, where the idea of Scotch conjures up strong and deeply held associations. In Taiwan though, it was novel and interesting, rather than odd and uncomfortable. Matisse quickly destroyed the previous market leader's dominant position to become the top whisky brand in that market.

The fact is, that coffee (or anything else for that matter) can be to the Chinese whatever they decide it's going to be.

This is often overlooked but matters because it can represent enormous opportunity.

Transcript
   Spilling the beans on China's coffee culture
   Broadcast on 2 February 2021
   Hosted by Bessie Lee, Jennie Liu

Guest
   Hou Yongpu (侯永璞) founded Yongpu coffee in 2014. In 2021 the brand secured 50 million yuan in series A+ funding and grew sales from RMB 20 million to RMB 100 million in 12 months. Sales now stand at RMB 400 million, making Yongpu the highest selling liquid coffee on Tmall.

Today, coffee has become much more ubiquitous and affordable in China with the arrival of coffee players including Luckin Coffee, convenience stores, fast-food chains and specialty coffee start-ups.

Packaged coffee products are no longer just "3-in-1" instant coffee in this coffee boom. The market is packed with freeze-dried coffee powder, coffee concentrate, drip bag coffee and many more forms. Although they are still labelled as instant and convenient, we have to admit these products can be as good as freshly ground coffee.

In this episode of Beiwanglu, we have invited Hou Yongpu, founder of Yongpu Coffee, to share his stories, insights into the specialty instant coffee market, and how coffee consumption in China has changed over the years.

Jenny

Today, we welcome Hou Yongpu, the founder of Yongpu Coffee, a new consumer coffee brand that many of us are very familiar with. It is currently one of the best-selling coffee brands on e-commerce platforms. They focused on premium instant coffee, such as liquid coffee concentrate, freeze-dried coffee and drip-bag coffee, which are pretty popular among young people.

Hou Yongpu

Hello everyone.

Jennie

You graduated from the China Academy of Art, and we know you were a graphic designer back then. Can you share with us your motivation for creating Yongpu Coffee?

Hou Yongpu

I liked coffee a lot when I was in college. At that time, I didn't know much about coffee and just drank a lot.

One day, I found a book about coffee planting in the library, and I felt deeply attracted to it because I have a natural affinity with farming as a countryside boy. So I have a natural affinity with farming.

It was fascinating for me to see how coffee was cultivated. I formed a completely different feeling for coffee, and my love for coffee moved to the next level.

Wouldn't it be nice if I could make coffee part of my career?

In my senior year, everyone was thinking about future career plans. I also considered just finding a designer job after graduation. But starting my own business was always my dream. After some consideration, I decided that making coffee should be something I would do for a long time. That's how I entered the coffee industry.

Jennie

In 2014, China's coffee market was more about low-end instant powder. What was the market like when you established your company?

What kind of difficulties have you encountered when you first established Yongpu Coffee? And did you find it challenging to educate the market?

Hou Yongpu

Before I established Yongpu, I worked in the coffee industry for nearly four years. When I graduated in 2009 and joined Mingqian Coffee in Shanghai in 2010 as a designer. At that time, the whole coffee market was still in its early stage.

After four years of working in Mingqian, I felt that it was time and established my own coffee brand.

In the beginning, we wanted our product to be easy to drink. Since we only had 300,000 yuan of start-up funds, we had to work out where our products should start. Drip bag coffee already existed on the market at that time, but it was challenging to promote it. From market research feedback, we found many customers just put the drip bag coffee in the water like a teabag. Back then, it was a huge task to educate the market.

Jennie

So at that time, most of the packaged coffee on the market were either instant coffee or drip bag coffee, right?

Hou Yongpu

Yes, because our goal is to make premium coffee, the only product type we could choose was drip bag coffee.

Jennie

Nowadays, we can find all types of coffee on the market. Like typical drip bag coffee, cold brew coffee bags that are good for summer, ice drip coffee, and better quality ones like freeze-dried coffee. Can you share with us what the differences are?

Hou Yongpu

Sure, if you enjoy drinking brewed coffee or black coffee, drip bag coffee is a good choice.

But from the perspective of a product manager, we consider drip bag coffee a niche product. The drip bag coffee is better at presenting the flavour of good coffee, but you need hot water for brewing, and you can only drink it black. Adding milk is not common for drip bag coffee.

You also need to consider the water temperature for the brew, ideally around 85-95 degrees.

The coffee bag is similar to drip bag coffee, it's just a lazier way of getting a coffee which is almost as good. The extraction is a little less good, because the contact between coffee and water is less direct.

We think liquid coffee concentrate is a good solution. It dissolves fast in water, milk and sparkling water. Allowing consumers to get a cup of coffee fast and easy, with excellent flavour retention. In our opinion, freeze-dried coffee is a transitional product that can be stored at an ambient temperature. In 2017, we made the first instant cold brew coffee liquid concentrate in China. The downside is it needs to be refrigerated. We tried to make it suitable for storing at room temperature.

Freeze-dried coffee is another good transitional solution. It can be stored at room temperature and ideal for brewing with water or milk, and it dissolves relatively fast with a few stirs. Because you still need to stir it in the brewing process, it still needs some improvement on user experience. If we can improve it and make it suitable for room temperature storage, it would be more convenient for our customers.

As a manufacturer, it is difficult for us to directly compare the costs of drip bag coffee, freeze-dried coffee, and liquid coffee concentrate. The production cost of drip bag coffee is mostly the cost of coffee beans, and the production cost of freeze-dried coffee is mostly spent on the processing. As for the liquid coffee concentrate, the production cost is spent on the coffee beans and processing.

. . .

Jennie

Which of them has the best potential to present a good flavour similar to a cup of freshly ground coffee?

Hou Yongpu

It should be drip bag coffee. Essentially, it is ground coffee bean powder brewed with hot water directly, but there is one consumer demand drip-bag coffee doesn't offer which is that many Chinese customers like to add milk to coffee.

Jennie

Based on your observation, which kind of coffee sells best among coffee products that occupied the largest market share? Or which type of coffee consumers are willing to buy more often?

Hou Yongpu

The best-selling product is freeze-dried coffee, and many brands are making it. Right now, freeze-dried coffee sells better than liquid coffee concentrate. But we predict liquid coffee concentrate will take over and become number one in two years.

To make freeze-dried coffee, we first need to extract liquid coffee from a coffee powder and water mixture, then feed the liquid coffee into a freeze-drying machine. Vacuum it while lowering temperature rapidly to -50°C when the coffee droplet has frozen into ice. Then the solid water becomes gaseous water and evaporates via sublimation. The inherent soluble material left behind is freeze-dried coffee. This process is both energy and time-consuming. It takes up to 24 hours for this process. And that's the reason why the production cost of freeze-dried coffee is high.

Interestingly, liquid coffee concentrate is an intermediate product before making freeze-dried coffee. So why is everyone more willing to make freeze-dried coffee? The answer is we all wanted to make liquid coffee concentrate, but there is an incredibly high technical barrier when making this product suitable for storing at room temperature. The core reason is that it's prone to breeding bacteria when there is still moisture. Freeze-dried coffee is easy to preserve because water has been removed. And now the challenge is you have to make it taste good without adding preservatives.

Till now, no other domestic companies have made significant progress on this matter except us. We worked with a family factory in Japan with over 70 years of history and solved this problem. After that, we launched the ambient temperature flash brew coffee to the market.

Bessie

What is the consumer insight in a booming market segment like instant drip bag coffee?

Hou Yongpu

We have coffee available everywhere. But in my opinion, maybe it's just the case in Shanghai only. It's not that ubiquitous in other cities. In the entire domestic market, there are four core consumer demands.

First, it has to be cheap. We are not talking about dirt

cheap prices like one or two yuan, but high cost-performance value.

Second, it has to be convenient. For example, a few years ago, when Luckin Coffee came out, what was their strategy? They claimed they have the same supply chain as Starbucks, the same coffee beans, even the same equipment. They said they produce the same quality coffee as Starbucks, but way cheaper and more convenient. When you place an order in their app, they will deliver the coffee to you within half an hour. That's where Luckin Coffee shines, being cheap and convenient.

Convenience store coffee is cheaper than Starbucks, at a price range of 10-15 yuan. They are also implementing the concept of convenience. So when we go to the convenience store to buy something, we might also grab a cup of coffee from there.

Manner coffee, a popular brand in Shanghai, has the same concept, a 10-15 yuan coffee in the office building, easy access for people working there.

Besides the demands of cheapness and convenience, the other demand is health. Why has Nescafe 3-in-1 coffee become less attractive now? Despite the fact that it's very cheap and convenient? because it's unhealthy.

The fourth and last demand is a good flavour.

It may be subjective, but I guess most of us agree Nescafe 3-in-1 is not tasty. We see many internet celebrity brands quietly disappearing after their first half-year recently. Why did they disappear? Because their products are not good enough, not tasty enough for consumers to buy them repeatedly.

In the domestic market, we think the consumers' four demands for coffee are low price, convenience, health, and good taste. As long as a product can meet these four criteria, it will be high in demand.

Bessie

In this context, healthy demand means the extraction process of instant coffee?

Hou Yongpu

We can simply understand it as whether it is zero sugar and zero fat from the ingredient list.

Jennie

We mentioned convenience store coffee and Luckin Coffee. Freshly ground coffee in these franchises is usually sold for around 10 to 20 yuan.

In the future, assuming that food delivery will become more convenient, especially in first-tier cities, and you can also easily buy 5 to 10 yuan freshly ground coffee, will there be an impact on the packaged coffee market?

Hou Yongpu

We think that's a good thing. There is still a lot of work to do on educating our domestic market. In our view, all coffee brands are educating the market and cultivating user consumption habits.

We have been talking about an obvious demand of young consumers. They enjoy pleasure in life. People are willing to find something delicious that meets their particular taste.

For example, when we order a cup of milk tea with many options available. You can choose from adding milk or oat milk, more sugar or less, and so on. Vendors are willing to provide such options to meet the demands of their consumers.

We see as a common practice recently that most vendors, whether it's the café downstairs or a convenience store, want to ensure the consistent quality of their coffee. Each cup of coffee should have the same taste.

But our goal is that we want to meet our customers' personalised preferences. For example, our customers often share their creative ways of enjoying our products on social media. Like pairing it with milk, oat milk, or a particular brand of milk, even sparkling water, which is a trendy option in summer.

Say you want to have a cold sparking coffee drink desperately on a hot summer day, and you ordered one online. All the bubbles are gone when it arrives, and the coffee is not so cold. Then you go to the café downstairs and try buying one from there, but it's pretty expensive. Alternatively, you can buy a bottle of sparkling water and a shot of our liquid coffee concentrate. It will just cost you 10 yuan. And there you have a cup of nice and cold sparkling coffee drink. Such enjoyment and experience are difficult to achieve in takeaways and cafes.

Bessie

I want to ask you about coffee drinking habits in China.

Some statistics show Chinese consumed on average 7.2 cups of coffee per capita in 2019. Of course, it's a bit low considering our large population base. When compared to 2013, it was only 3.2 cups. It's already more than double the growth. When we compare with other countries, like the United States, which consumes 388 cups, the data from 2018, we are about 7 cups at the time, so the room for growth must be enormous.

Since China has always been a tea-drinking culture country, do you think coffee consumption has any potential to reach the level of Europe or the United States?

Or, more realistically, reach half of their amount, any possibility?

Hou Yongpu

I don't think we need to wait to reach half of their consumption. If we can achieve 1/10, that would be an outstanding achievement, considering China's huge population base. We can definitely see that day coming.

And we see many social media accounts promoting the health benefits of drinking black coffee. We also see that more and more young people are starting to drink coffee.

Our current marketing goal is to attract more new customers in the age group of 18-24. We have a saying in the industry that whoever masters the taste demand of the young will succeed in the future.

These potential customer groups will grow larger and larger in the future. As income grows, people find themselves increasingly able to afford coffee. When I had just graduated from school, a cup of coffee cost more than 30 yuan. And the income was so low, so was the housing price. Back then, we felt drinking coffee gave you a kind of prestige. Only very few people can afford it. But now we consider coffee as an ordinary drink. So naturally, more and more people will start to drink coffee.

. . .

Jennie

The Chinese Coffee Market Report from Mintel Group Ltd mentioned that Chinese consumers have always preferred latte over Americano. Black coffee is not so popular in China, but everyone likes latte. You also said that Chinese people tend to add milk while making coffee at home. Why is there such a consumption habit? And generally, coffee with milk is trendy in China. It has a relatively large market share.

Hou Yongpu

We can see the same thing with tea. Which one sells better? The original leaf tea or milk tea? Definitely milk tea, right?

People have a natural affinity with dairy products. They have always felt that coffee should be paired with milk when you consider that those coffee brands always put coffee and milk together in their commercials in the early days. It was the same situation for many chocolate brands. Back then, society promoted milk as a very good thing, and people developed an inherent impression that milk is fragrant, especially combined with coffee.

As for black coffee, frankly speaking, I think it's very difficult for anyone to start their coffee drinking experience from a cup of black coffee. So, it's quite reasonable to add milk to coffee.

In the next ten years, China's coffee market will be for coffee beverages.

That's probably why Nongfu Spring (a Chinese bottled water and beverage company) has launched a sparkling coffee drink, "Tanbing", that has drawn a lot of attention and discussions.

. . .

Bessie

You mentioned that your marketing goal is to attract more young customers, especially new customers. This group of people has a lot of things that they want to try. And other businesses also see them as potential customers and try to instil new consumption habits in them.

With all these consumer products targeting this group of people, you are fighting a share of wallet war. That means they can choose to drink HeyTea (a milk tea retail brand), or they can choose to buy milk coffee or milk tea from a supermarket or convenience store. From your perspective, how do you make a breakthrough and convince consumers to choose your product over others?

Hou Yongpu

In China, there is a natural advantage for coffee when compared with tea. People feel coffee is a more quality drink than others. As for how to get more milk tea drinkers to switch to coffee, thanks to Luckin Coffee and their crazy subsidies. It made people feel like that they were losing out big time if they did not drink a cup of their latte every day. So Luckin Coffee has contributed a lot to the Chinese coffee market, helping it go through the tough early stage of market development.

That said, this particular mark is very early stage and foreign business owners might actually want to wait until different segments emerge over time.

To enter China, you either already have something which the Chinese value in terms of reputation (style and food from Italy, tailoring & etiquette from England, wines from France).

Jennie

So, was coffee's advantage in China related to the 3rd wave of coffee? Like the concept called the 3rd space promoted by Starbucks. It feels more formal to meet someone at a coffee place.

Hou Yongpu

Yes, I think this is the crucial early educational marketing Starbucks has done in China. When I first came to Shanghai after graduating from school, people felt great when they had a Starbucks coffee in their hands. Of course, we don't have that kind of feeling anymore.

Jennie

I have another question. As mentioned before, Nongfu Spring is starting to sell RTD (ready to drink) coffee. And since Yongpu Coffee doesn't have this product line right now, do you plan to make it in the future? And what's the advantage of RTD coffee products? Why are the big companies entering this market segment?

Hou Yongpu

I think big companies are doing it just to occupy the market position for the future. Or they have too many resources and just want to spend some on RTD coffee and see how it will work out. I'm not a big fan of RTD coffee, personally.

As we mentioned before, Chinese consumers usually prefer latte. When we check the same type of product in RTD coffee, usually advertised as latte or mocha, these products have a very long ingredient list. That means many kinds of additives and milk powder have been added. It has to be milk powder. There are technical barriers to using fresh milk directly.

All these additives and milk powder are added to ensure the liquid mixture reaches a balance point so that no reaction occurs and the product can be stored at ambient temperature for 6-9 months. It's not so much a healthy drink. It goes against the four key demands we mentioned earlier. Also, it's not cheap. It usually costs around 10 yuan or more. Why not choose freshly brewed coffee rather than a can of coffee full of additives and without real milk?

Jennie

Some of the specialty coffee brands that have emerged from coffee shops are also starting to launch their own RTD coffee products. Generally, it's a product that features short shelf life, no sugar, mostly black coffee, or something with a relatively shorter ingredient list.

When I talked to one of the brands, they told me that making RTD coffee is quite challenging for a small company like them.

I'm curious whether the big companies will follow up on producing this kind of healthier coffee with less or no sugar? Will there be a potential market? And what are the challenges of making RTD coffee?

. . .

Hou Yongpu

If the company you spoke with is still selling the RTD coffee, I guess it would be very difficult for them now.

To my understanding, the challenge of making RTD coffee is the minimum order quantity. To make this kind of product, you need to use large equipment and produce a huge amount in one batch.

If they decide to make a short shelf-life product, there must be many unsold items after the shelf-life runs out. If they decide to make a long shelf-life product, it won't be any better. I have talked with a large manufacturing company and know that for one batch of a single flavour order, the minimum order quantity requires almost one million cans, and it has to be produced in one batch.

These one million cans of coffee will take up a lot of storage space and occupy a large amount of working capital. How can we sell these one million cans of coffee in four months just by ourselves? The shelf life is only nine months.

This is very difficult for start-ups, almost an impossible mission. For a big company like Nongfu Spring, they don't mind the waste. With their vast distribution network, one million cans are just a small number that can be sold in 1 or 2 months. Compared to their vast sales revenue, they could just ignore it.

Bessie

It's a trend that the younger generation emphasises individual personality more than ever. The case for coffee is that it can have many options.

For example, for a cup of simple latte, you can add different amounts of milk of different kinds, like regular milk, low-fat, milk or plant milk. Add sugar or without, brown sugar or white sugar.

Each person's habit is different. Yongpu Coffee is getting more and more successful in the market. The key reason is that the younger generation will prefer to have a cup of coffee that suits their particular taste over a mass-produced regular coffee off the shelf.

Do these standardised products go against young people's wishes of pursuing personalisation?

Hou Yongpu

No. It is a future trend that more young people are looking for personalised products. But at the same time, high-quality standardised products will still be in demand. Take Manner Coffee in Shanghai, for example. They have kept their coffee at a consistently high standard. There is a large group of people who like pure and simple things. When they have a good latte, they also want to have the same good latte tomorrow.

The demand for personalised taste is a future trend, but the next question is, how is the trend going to be? Compared to people who don't like changes, will there be more or fewer of them? My judgment is there will be more of them (people who prefer personalised products). It might take five years or even ten years to get there. We have to look further into the future since we are a start-up company.

Bessie

What is the concept behind the packaging of your products?

...

Hou Yongpu

I think every start-up company will inherently have a strong influence from its founder. Because of my designer background, our products will focus more on design. A founder with a science background probably pays more attention to theories and data.

The first product of Yongpu is a co-branded product that we created with an illustrator. In 2015, barely any brands in China made co-branded products. Choosing this model doesn't mean it's good, but we don't have any other option. We only had 300,000 yuan as initial capital. After we set up the office, paid the rent, and decided drip bag coffee would be our first product, we found the remaining money was only enough for the first batch of products. What can we do?

I knew a lot of illustrators. They also like coffee, and their user stickiness is very strong. I often joke with my illustrator friends, "When will you make your illustrations into products?"

So I asked myself, why not use this resource and find an illustrator to create a co-branded product? So I contacted the founder of Xiaozaizi's Theatre. At that time, his WeChat emoji series was very popular, and he had many fans. Then I met him and told him that I wanted to create a co-branded coffee with him.

Our first product was launched online on 15 January. We only had a Taobao store back then because we were not qualified to open a Tmall store yet. Xiaozaizi's Theatre shared a post on their official account about this first peripheral product, an especially good coffee. Anyone who wants to try it can buy it from the Yongpu online store.

That night the sales revenue was more than 20,000 yuan. That was a fortune for us then.

After the first attempt, I found that with zero promotion cost, our partner gets his own product, we get traffic and sales. Such a win-win solution. We had no reason to stop.

Later on, we cooperated with Cat's Kitchen (a food vlogger channel), I can I BB (an online debate variety show in China), and others.

Between 2014 to 2019, we did about 300-400 cases of co-branded products. Choosing co-branding allows us to survive in the early days. And we kept a very high standard for each case on packaging design.

When we decided to make freeze-dried coffee, Saturnbird had already launched their signature small-cup packaging. I told myself that we couldn't be a copycat. We had to hold on to our designing principle, and we shouldn't become followers.

Then we spent half a year designing a small flying saucer. But we found the moulding factory couldn't do it. Making the small flying saucer, they need to use the injection moulding process, which will have an injection point on the surface. For example, take a good look at the Saturnbird's small-cup style package. You will find its lid and jar have an injection point. Our flying saucer has a very round and smooth surface. An injection point on the surface is unacceptable.

Then we consulted with ten more moulding factories. One of them said they could do it, though costly. We had no choice but to do it. It's such a challenging task, but we solved it within two months of trial and error. The injection point was moved to the inside of the flying saucer in the end. The outcome seems good and consumers like it.

. . .

Bessie

So this is where the flying saucer style packaging came from. And no matter who you co-branded with, the product package will be the same shape.

I see that your recent co-branding with Xiaoyuzhou (a popular podcast app) also features a flying saucer shape.

Hou Yongpu

Recently, a user shared a picture in the chat group. I feel quite touched by it. It's his friend's collection of all the freeze-dried coffee on the market, with dozens of Freeze-dried coffee brands. All these brands use the same small-cup style packaging except ours. People who are not familiar with it will probably think it's from the same company. Only our flying saucer stands out.

Jennie

So the flying saucer packaging could help your brand better compete with other emerging consumer brands?

Speaking of Saturnbird, it seems more and more players are entering this market segment. In addition to the packaging, what is the other core competence of the brand?

Hou Yongpu

I think the competitiveness of a brand is never just a single aspect. It is more multi-dimensional. A good packaging design could be part of the answer. But how effective is it? It still depends on whether the packaging can be easily copied.

You can find a lot of Saturnbird small-cup style packaging copycats on the market, which means its design is easily duplicated. It is a relatively weak barrier against copycats. When we designed our flying saucer, we also integrated a unique differentiator with it - our mascot Shiduanzheng (a cartoon-style stone lion figure). All of our packages will feature Shiduanzheng. This combination will make it more costly for anyone who wants to copy it.

I think appearance is one aspect, and it also depends on whether it's easy to copy. Another part of the barrier is the product itself.

We are now the only company in China that sells ambient temperature flash brew coffee. It has a very high technical barrier. Right now, no factory in China can make it. But this technical barrier will not be there forever. We may see it disappear in 1-2 years.

Another long-term barrier is the brand concept we gradually convey to our consumers. For example, we define ourselves as an interesting and heartwarming coffee brand. Our mascot Shiduanzheng is an embodiment of this concept. The core is how the brand conveys its ideas to the consumers.

Bessie

So is there any special reason for you to choose flying saucers as the packaging style? And is there anything to do with the concept of Coffee Planet?

Hou Yongpu

Well, that's a long story. At the time, we had a super ambitious slogan, 'Nice coffee of the universe.' *(Editor's* note: this, like many excellent Chinese brand names and slogans doesn't survive translation.)

We wanted to create a brand culture featuring a concept of the universe. For example, we had a pretty interesting product series called 'Planet Project.' The season one product was a collection of drip bag coffee from seven specialty coffee brands in China. It includes every brand's signature coffee flavour. We cooperated with five specialty coffee brands from Taiwan in season two and created the series called 'grey dot bag', very similar to drip bag coffee but in a round shape. Each grey dot bag represents the signature flavour of one brand.

That's how we implemented the concept of Coffee Planet and where the slogan 'Nice coffee of the universe' came from. It is the direction we are working on. And later on, we have the flying saucer.

Bessie

Very ambitious ideas, to make the best coffee in the universe.

Hou Yongpu

Yes, the best coffee in the universe. We just need to remove the 'best' statement in commercials. Otherwise, it's a violation of the Chinese advertising law. So we're saying 'Nice coffee of the universe' instead. It's on the edge of the law. Ha ha.

Bessie

So you've done more than 400 co-brandings in the past

six years. It sounds like the very popular DTC (direct to consumer) model in recent years. To select partners from small start-ups who might also be at the bottleneck of expanding users and then co-branding with them, especially those who can do DTC. Is taking small steps and accumulating customers gradually this way a good choice of brand and business development for a start-up brand?

Hou Yongpu

Yes. The most important fact is that co-branding helped us survive in the early days. It allowed us to slowly open up our brand to the market and let more users know us.

Our development is quite slow at this stage. Until the end of 2015, our sales were less than 2 million yuan. Major development happened in 2020. By that time, we had much better products and had begun to capitalise. The main benefit of co-branding is that it helped us survive the early days.

Now we have more resources. This allows us to do more interesting things with co-branding and try our innovative ideas. There are a lot of co-branded products on the market, mostly pretty standardised. So we explored the possibility of scaling up the campaign, putting it online, and associating with dozens of brands together simultaneously.

In May 2020, we planned a campaign on Weibo to cooperate with 36 brands. Each day we communicated with one of the brands online. And they would take out their most exciting products for fans to interact with. All these 36 brands got a relatively large online exposure. It was so successful that many media selected the campaign as the online marketing case of the month. And we further magnified this activity during the annual online shopping festival of double eleven (11 November). It became a co-branding of 60 brands. Our influence gets even bigger. By our calculation, we get 20 to 30 million brand mentions on social media at the cost of merely 30,000-40,000 yuan. All our partner brands, including us, got a relatively large amount of free traffic. We consider this the most interesting co-branding event in 2020.

Bessie

I'm curious when you do co-branding, you have to cooperate with other brands or platforms. How did you remain true to yourself when you work with other brands with distinctive personalities, tones and images?

Especially when you only have very low visibility in the early stage, is it possible that after more than 400 co-branded product cases, some of your old customers will get confused about what kind of brand Yongpu is? And will your brand positioning be affected by these brands you are co-branding with?

Hou Yongpu

Yes, it does. That's precisely the pain point.

In the early days, the positioning of our brand was very vague. People would view us as a good-looking brand.

Too often, many of our gorgeous items were co-branded. Our own products don't have many characteristics. So we saw co-branding as essential to staying alive. At that time, the first thing to consider was survival. Then you can have the chance and right to talk about brand positioning. We finally started to develop our brand characteristics for Yongpu in the second half of 2019.

The first thing we did was to create our brand mascot Shiduanzheng. Then we changed the old packaging to the new one, with all of them featuring Shiduanzheng. And we also adjusted the ratio of co-branded products vs our original products to 20%: 80% on our online shop. Gradually, our brand characteristics became clearer. But without those early-stage co-brandings, we couldn't have survived, let alone get to creating all these things.

Bessie

You said that you have to be very realistic when starting your own business. If you don't survive, all your dreams and visions are useless. Survive first, then feel your way out. People who have experience on this matter will resonates.

I saw many co-branding cases, and most of them usually choose to cooperate with KOL or a famous influencer on the big platform. Yet you decided to collaborate with Xiaoyuzhou, a pretty new field as a popular podcast app in China. We are running a podcast, so it's natural to think that everyone around us is listening to podcast. In reality, the majority of people don't.

When you choose to listen to a podcast, you are either in a quiet place or wearing noise-cancelling earphones somewhere. In this immersive private world, I feel coffee and podcasts are a perfect match in this unique and private moment.

Hou Yongpu

I totally agree.

. . .

As for podcast listeners, they have developed a strong sense of intimacy and trust with the podcast they like. Brand names that have been mentioned and products that have been highly recommended in the podcasts, these listeners will develop a strong sense of confidence in them. An intimate voice in your ear feels close and trustworthy. So I believe the podcast industry will have a prosperous future. I need to listen to more podcasts in the future. Otherwise, I will get further away from understanding young people and what they like.

Bessie

Because Yongpu had already built up its reputation, it has a very positive brand image. By the way, I like that mascot. I guess now others are lining up trying to do co-branding with you. Your standard of choosing partners must be stricter than before. Now, on what condition will you agree to a co-branding campaign with another brand? Or what criteria other brands have to meet to co-brand with Yongpu?

Hou Yongpu

For me, it's whether we can have a mutual understanding.

Once we meet and talk, I can feel whether we are on the same page. If we share the same goal to do co-branding well, that's what we are willing to do. On the other hand, if the goal is to make money, it would not be a good collaboration.

Co-branding is not something you can make money from. It's time-consuming and costly. For us, it is a fun thing to do. If we get along with each other, we can explore the possibilities. An ideal partner is someone who is willing to work with us to make co-branding fun.

Bessie

So the partner doesn't need to be a big brand, as long as you are both willing to explore how to make the product fun. The most important thing is both parties need to have compatible brand ideas and incentives to do a fun project.

Hou Yongpu

Yes, many big brands are willing to cooperate with us now. But we still need to remain true to our original aspiration. Doing fun projects is always a priority for co-branding.

We have recently discussed how much energy and time we should spend on co-branding. After all, our energy and time are limited. Maybe 2-3 cases per month of co-branding will be a reasonable number. But we did 7-8 cases. It seems a bit too much for our team.

Jennie

Maybe it's time for you to go your own way now.

Hou Yongpu

After we have raised funding from VC, sales become a crucial KPI, and if we put more effort into our products, we can generate more revenue. Co-branding is a plus, but we still need to balance between doing fun projects and running the main business. With too many co-branding cases, our team will get tired, which will further affect other projects' efficiency. The overall effect of co-branding will have some negative impacts too.

Jennie

I heard Yongpu Coffee got its own coffee plantation in 2019 and secured a raw coffee bean supply. I'm curious, are there many new coffee consumer brands that have their own coffee plantations like yours? This kind of asset-heavy model, with its own factory, equipment, and plantation? Is this going to be a critical path for the emergence of new consumer coffee brands by moving from light assets to heavy assets?

Hou Yongpu

There are not many brands that have their own coffee plantation. It's more like an optional thing. It depends on their brand positioning.

The raw coffee bean trade is already a very mature industry. It's not a requirement to use raw coffee beans from our plantation. Having our coffee plantation is for the consideration of brand building.

In 2019, we found an interesting thing: many people in China know about Blue Mountain coffee but have never drunk real Blue Mountain coffee. We happened to talk to some traders from Japan about this. They said they could take us to Jamaica to see the Blue Mountain coffee plantations there and maybe also consider co-operation if we are interested.

We went there, and I really liked it. We also learned

how they produce good quality Blue Mountain coffee. What I admire most is the way they consider sustainability in the whole production process.

After harvest, the coffee beans have to go through an essential processing step. It involves using a lot of water, which becomes acidic after it's soaked with coffee beans. I know a lot of plantations are discharging wastewater directly into the river or soil, and over time the environment is destroyed.

Here in Blue Mountain coffee plantation, they spend a lot of money recycling all the wastewater. After that, the water can be reused or discharged safely.

They also planted many plants and vegetables in addition to coffee in their plantation. Their concern for sustainability surprised me.

That was the first time I heard that coffee plantations were willing to spend such big money to do things like this.

So we had a conversation on how we see Blue Mountain coffee in China and potential co-operation opportunities on the coffee plantation. They are the largest plantation owners in Jamaica, owning about 17 or 18 plantations.

We asked to become a contractor for one plantation. We would buy all the raw beans, and we also like to name the plantation. At first, they didn't agree. Then we invited them to China to visit the world's largest coffee exhibition held every April in Shanghai. They came to China and visited our company. They seemed to like our company culture - many young people and innovative product designs. And they viewed us as a coffee brand for young people.

We had a very nice and frank conversation. They gave us the plantation we wanted. It's much easier than I anticipated. I even told them that I couldn't pay them right away due to a lack of money. In the end, we signed a 10-year contract. And that was how we obtained the Blue Mountain coffee plantation.

Later on, we developed our high-end line called Doctor Bird, and then the Blue Mountain cold brew liquid and the Blue Mountain drip bag coffee. They are all very popular. The feedback and reviews on our Tmall store showed that consumers found the products "delicious and expensive". And those consumers were also buying it repeatedly.

That's the reason why we need to own a coffee plantation.

Jennie

I noticed that many consumers now prefer to choose coffee products with a 'Fair-trade' mark in Europe and the United States. What's the concept of the 'Fair-trade' mark? And why does it matter in commodity trade?

Hou Yongpu

We can simply understand it as that we are willing to pay more to buy farmers' coffee. The extra money goes to projects that help them to improve their lives and local cultivation techniques.

It is an issue of environmental sustainability. If the farmers' incomes are too low, they will not be so dedicated to planting coffee. If the local environment worsens, they can't process the coffee properly. So it's a concept of promoting sustainability.

Bessie

A lot of agricultural products are starting to implement this 'Fair-trade' concept.

In these past decades, large enterprises have been expanding into more and more areas. They are all inclined to lower the cost to the minimum. Because of that, farmers earn very little from a year of hard work. The big companies took most of the profits.

After so many decades of exploitation, many farmers began to unite, and then slowly, the concept of 'Fair-trade' emerged, and now there is an association promoting the idea.

There are many commodities with 'Fair-trade' marks on the European and American markets. If your product belongs to the Fair-trade system, its retail price will be slightly higher. Many consumers in Europe and the United States are willing to pay extra for these Fair-trade products because it protects farmers' interests.

This is the concept of the 'Fair-trade' and how it begins.

Hou Yongpu

Some specialty coffee producers in China, like Seesaw Coffee and Manner Coffee, are doing similar things in Yunnan, China.

Yunnan is a place that has the best resources to produce coffee, and its advantages are quite significant compared to other coffee origins in the world.

Because some large companies have been purchasing raw materials at low prices in Yunnan for years, local farmers have little incentive to grow coffee well.

Some specialty coffee producers like us will go to Yunnan and work with farmers directly. A coffee plantation in Baoshan (a city in Yunnan province) that we cooperated with has a piece of land contracted to us. Farmers will grow coffee with our requirements. Then we buy all the coffee beans at a higher price. I hope such efforts can help improve the quality of Yunnan coffee.

But improving coffee bean quality cannot be done in the short term. It may take 3-5 years, ten years, or even a longer time. I'm still optimistic about it. The reason behind my optimism is that many of our industry peers are socially responsible and willing to do their part for developing Yunnan's coffee industry. That is the part I felt most touched.

Bessie

That is a great demonstration of corporate responsibility.

For our audience who want to know more, I recommend a documentary series on Netflix called Rotten. It's about the agricultural industry, how big companies exploit farmers. One of the episodes is about the coffee industry, and I highly recommend our audience to watch that episode. You'll be shocked to learn how farmers lived under immense pressure from the big companies and how struggling they are in their daily lives.

We hope to support the 'Fair-trade' movement more so that this concept can flourish in China.

Jennie

I want to ask why Yunnan coffee beans are so cheap. I know Seesaw coffee, Starbucks, and some other specialty coffee brands have done a lot of work in Yunnan related to purchasing and producing raw coffee beans.

What is the reason that the overall price of Yunnan coffee beans is lower than that of the Ethiopian?

Hou Yongpu

I think it still depends on the willingness of the local people. If they put effort and investment in growing good coffee, it is possible to have a good outcome. But the current market price doesn't allow people to plant coffee with care. When the farmers end up with a low income, it's not sustainable, no matter how passionate they are.

That's why many of our peers are willing to buy high-quality raw materials that meet their requirements at a higher price. Farmers will gradually recognise that there is a good margin to make growing good quality coffee.

Regarding the idea of good coffee from Yunnan, there has been a big change in the last three to five years. Starbucks has built a huge art device in front of its flagship store in 2020, featuring Yunnan coffee and trying to convey to their customers that there is good coffee in Yunnan. Manner coffee also buys raw materials from Yunnan in large quantities. And we have cold brew coffee liquid products from Yunnan. Consumers can get their hands on good coffee from Yunnan easily now.

We are all working in this direction to let more people know that there is good coffee in Yunnan. It may take a long time, but when we look back five years later, we will feel all these things are meaningful.

Bessie

The Fair-trade movement can return more profits to the farmers. It is expected that after the farmers' incomes have improved, they are more likely to invest in environmental protection.

Like the Blue Mountain plantations you mentioned earlier, they will invest a lot of money in wastewater recycling and treatment instead of discharging directly and polluting the environment. The Fair-trade Association has this kind of requirement for these crop producers. I am very impressed to hear that you and your peers are already doing this in Yunnan.

———

3
SURVIVE AND THRIVE IN A CHINA START-UP

Now for the most entertaining & insightful of all the episodes presented here, at least in our opinion.

Wu Xiaobo, our guest, is a major celebrity in the Chinese business world; the author of multiple best-selling books, founder of many successful new businesses, talent spotter and observer-cum-angel investor for 20 or more each year.

Nominally, this is an episode about digitalisation and its importance to Chinese entrepreneurs, both on the demand and supply side.

But Mr Wu's major interest is on seeking to explain why the Chinese market and, especially, the Chinese character, are so well suited to entrepreneurialism and for us, this is where the episode offers most insight.

Mr Wu states that "China is probably the best country in the world for start-ups". We agree but think it's helpful to delve further into why that should be. Let's start with the most straightforward, the sheer size of the market.

China actually has substantial variation in local culture

and language, with many local dialects, sometimes mutually incomprehensible. Yet all regions use the same characters and a majority of Chinese are 'bi-lingual', speaking their own dialect and Mandarin Chinese (strictly speaking Putonghua, or 'common speech').

Similarly, the legal system is common to all and more-or-less consistently applied across China. Most significantly perhaps, China has been a relative late comer to the world of modern commerce. As a result, it has skipped several development stages and adopted modern digital communication, e-commerce and social media systems wholesale.

What we have in practice then is a very large 'local' market in which businesses and consumers can connect across vast distances with ease, speaking a common language and operating within a shared legal and regulatory system.

This is not merely convenient. Mr Wu makes the point that an online business which might never be capable of achieving profitable scale in other parts of the world can do so with relative ease in China by sheer dint of numbers.

This alone might justify Mr Wu's belief in the superiority of China as an incubator for new ventures, but in fact, we believe the most important factor is a by-product of Chinese culture and the character it has forged. Put simply, ordinary Chinese people have a genius for entrepreneurialism.

Resilience, fate and the Chinese character

Why should this be? Clearly the Chinese are people like the rest of us and don't possess superpowers. Yet there *is* something singular in the Chinese approach.

Mr Wu ascribes this entrepreneurial flair to an innate practicality, a materialist love of consumption and a predilection for gambling. These traits are real and observable, but why should the Chinese lean in this direction? To explain China's flair for business we need to know where these traits come from. As so often in China, the root causes lie in the past.

The culture that we in the West think of as 'Chinese' largely pre-dates the 20th Century and is, more correctly, the culture of China's ancient ruling classes. It's a culture of written language, historical record, administration, artistic & architectural achievement, philosophy, and correctness of ritual & deportment. This is all fascinating of course, but, it doesn't give much insight into the hearts, minds or lives of ordinary Chinese people.

In the West, our political class, however privileged, is essentially drawn from the same 'meme pool' as ourselves and views the world through a similar lens. This has become increasingly true with modernity. In contrast, as Chinese culture evolved, the imperial civil service system, with its onerous examinations and eight legged essays, marked a clear division between the gentry and ordinary citizens.

This cultural separation, coupled with China's size, complexity and vulnerability to natural disaster may explain the view that Chinese culture is 'collectivist'. Leadership had little option but focus on the greater good. For ordinary people living outside the administrative system however, life was perilous; a daily grind for subsistence, often conducted in the face of flood, drought, famine and plague.

Circumstances are very different today, but the people of modern China have inherited a terrific degree of mental toughness, self-sufficiency and an impressive ability to squeeze maximum benefit out of any given situation, no matter how challenging.

In terms of entrepreneurial start-ups, it's hardly a startling insight to suggest that resilience and adaptability are conducive to success. It's only half the story however.

The problem with flood, plague and famine is that no amount of resilience can guarantee survival. Over long generations, the Chinese have evolved coping-mechanisms; one of which, 'Guanxi', we've already discussed. Even more fundamental however, is an unshakeable belief in fate, something which is widely and profoundly held by ordinary Chinese even today.

Wu Xiaobo picks up on the Chinese predilection for gambling as evidence of an entrepreneurial mindset. We think rather that it's a function of their ingrained fatalism. Nobody hustles like a Chinese entrepreneur on the march, but nobody is more aware that the unforeseen will sometimes strike. Chinese business owners greet challenge or disaster with a shrug and an almost supernaturally swift pivot to a different, more effective approach.

There remains just one further point to make before moving onto the transcript of the episode, and it's to do with the unique circumstances facing China's young people.

Youthful Optimism

Any Chinese over the age of 50 remembers life in the late 60's and early 70's, a time of great turbulence and hardship. But for those in their 30's or below, the past really is a different country.

Mr Wu points out that younger Chinese are more naturally curious and creative and in this I suppose they are little different to young people anywhere in the world. They have also grown up in an era of increasing prosperity as China has sought to regain its position as a global force. Many are the children of the first wave of modern entrepreneurs who have built a more comfortable, sometimes seriously opulent life. They are far less affected, then, by the antagonistic forces which plagued earlier generations.

What's more, they are the immediate beneficiaries of an internet and telecoms powered economy more pervasive, coherently structured, complete and efficient than any in the world.

This is not to underestimate the challenges facing young Chinese, when leaving education, entering the workforce and generally starting out on adult life. But these challenges have themselves been a significant factor in turning young people towards entrepreneurialism and they have been quick to seize the opportunities for success which China's new economy offers.

Transcript:
    China's Start-Up Challenge
    Broadcast on 27 October 2021
    Hosted by Bessie Lee

. . .

Guest

Wu Xiaobo:

Highly respected Chinese economist, business writer, investor and entrepreneur. Author of several bestselling business books, including "The Great Defeat" and the 'Blue Lion" financial series.

Extensive experience in corporate research, visiting scholar at Harvard University & former professor of EMBA courses at Shanghai Jiao Tong and Jinan Universities.

There are more than 60 million micro and small businesses in China. That's equivalent to the population of the United Kingdom and still growing. According to a CASS (Chinese Academy of Social Sciences) survey, about 97% of start-ups will fail within 18 months.

How can so many small businesses and entrepreneurs survive given the extreme failure rate in this market?

In this episode of Beiwanglu, we have invited financial writer and business observer Wu Xiaobo to discuss the secret of business innovation for small businesses, digitalisation.

Although digitalisation is not a new concept in China, it is crucial for every entrepreneur to correctly understand and implement digital thinking to achieve adaptive innovation. Compared to large enterprises, small businesses are less resilient to risk in this post-epidemic era where the economy is in the doldrums. From small start-ups to design-intensive or compute-intensive small companies, they need innovative business strategies to survive in a fluctuating market. We hope this interview will provide more answers to our audience.

Wu Xiaobo has written many books on economic reform, China's opening-up in the past 40 years, and the evolution of enterprises. His books include China Emerging series, Lost Games I, Lost Games II, and Tencent, which describes the development of Tencent. He has a remarkable systematic observation of China's economic development. According to his team, he visits more than 50 companies every year to better understand the challenges, opportunities and situations they are facing. Today we are going to have a conversation with Wu Xiaobo about SMEs.

Small and medium-sized enterprises hold a vital position in China's national economy. They contribute more than 50% of tax revenue, 60% of the GDP, 70% of technological innovation, 80% of urban employment, and 90% of businesses. The recent Dell Digitalisation for Small Business white paper mentions that small businesses provide up to 420 million jobs at the end of 2020. That is why SMEs have had such a pivotal role in China's development over the past 40 years. But it's the large enterprises that get the most attention, while few people talk about SMEs. My own company is one of them.

Bessie

How are large, medium, small and micro enterprises defined in China? Are they any different from abroad?

Wu Xiaobo

In China, there is a business category for enterprises with an annual output value of 20 million RMB and above.

. . .

Bessie

Does 20 million RMB refer to revenue?

Wu Xiaobo

Yes, there are more than 12 million companies in this category in China. And there are over 60 million small and micro businesses and individual business owners in China, which is equivalent to the population of the UK.

Bessie

Yes, just over 67 million.

Wu Xiaobo

China also has the largest growth in the number of small and micro businesses in the world. Over the past ten years, there have been three to four million new micro and small businesses established in China each year, basically 10 000 start-ups every day. And 97% of them will close within 18 months.

Despite the risks, people still continue to start new businesses. (Humorously) Suicide can be triggered by many things, emotional problems for example, but in China, it's rarely caused by a failed business attempt. This shows that entrepreneurs are strong inside and can withstand the blow of failure.

What if they suffer a series of start-up failures? That would be even less likely to cause suicidal thoughts. Failing five times in business makes you a business mentor. Teaching the lessons of business failure can be one's own next business venture.

. . .

Bessie

Do you often deal with this type of entrepreneur?

Wu Xiaobo

Yes, I have encountered a lot of them in my daily life.

The barbershop I usually go to is a small start-up company. I have a fund dedicated to investing in start-ups, and I invest in roughly 20 to 30 of them every year.

Our team looks at some 2,000-3,000 start-ups and selects about 1% of them to invest in. These companies have a high failure rate. Even among those that receive our investment, the failure rate is about one third in the first few years. Those that can't get investment will almost definitely fail.

Starting a business is a risky activity. Many of my fans online ask me the first things to look for when starting a business. I told them they have to understand their start-ups are more likely to fail than succeed. Only when they can accept the reality that they might fail are they ready to start a business.

Bessie

Do you think the Chinese market is start-up-friendly to SMEs?

Wu Xiaobo

China is probably the best country in the world for start-ups.

Bessie

What's the reason? Because there are so many people in China? A large population base.

Wu Xiaobo

China is highly populated and the Chinese community tends to congregate together. There are 20 cities in China with over 10 million people, while in Europe, that might be a country's population. Many cities in Europe are so small that one mayor might govern only 80,000 citizens, which is probably less than the population of one of our street districts in Shanghai.

Bessie

Yes, you are right.

Wu Xiaobo

A massive population that cluster together over prolonged periods is a characteristic of China.

During the Han Dynasty, say around 100BC, China had a population of 50 million, and by 1000 AD, the Song Dynasty had a population of 100 million. By the end of the Qing Dynasty in 1900, there were 320 million people in China.

We all know that the more people there are, the easier it is to do business.

In addition, the Chinese people have two very interesting traits. The first is that we are pragmatic and materialistic.

There is a famous temple in Hangzhou called Lingyin, where most people make the same three wishes: wealth, safety and peace.

This kind of pragmatism is inherited from our Confucian culture. Being pragmatic means that we all love to consume, resulting in the development in all sectors of the market. For example, every region of China has its unique style of cuisine, and there are more than 50 different ways to play mah-jong. Hangzhou, Sichuan, Ningbo, and Shanghai all have different rules for the same game.

And secondly, Chinese people love gambling. The world's largest casino is in Macau, which generates six times the revenue of Las Vegas. And the Chinese contributed 60% of the turnover in Las Vegas.

In my study of China's 2000 years of business history, I found that no matter how big a disaster the country went through, even if the cities burned down and regimes toppled, once a new dynasty was established, society immediately entered a more productive era.

In five years, a village would be formed, then a market town in 10 years, and a city in 20 years, 30 years to become a prosperous society, and 50 years of peace was enough to make China the largest economy in the world at that point in time. This is equally true of China today, since the reform and opening up in 1978, to China becoming the world's largest economy sometime around 2028.

A large population base gives companies a substantial benefit, a domestic market that they are familiar with. Mercedes-Benz invented the first automobile in Germany in 1886. In the same year, Americans invented Coca-Cola, and after that, Detroit became the centre of automobile production. By 1908, the United States became the nation on wheels and took control of the automobile industry.

By 1978, the Japanese car production gradually caught up and eventually overtook the United States. It was in 2010 that China surpassed the United States in auto production. Japan's production was about six million cars per year when it overtook the United States. However, Japan's domestic market is too small for so many cars, and the industry had to rely on exports for growth.

Lexus, for example, is a brand that focuses on the European and US markets. China's 26 million vehicles are basically all sold domestically. About two million new energy vehicles were produced in China this year, accounting for half of the global production, also mostly sold in China. The huge domestic market from China's population base is a special advantage for individual business start-ups as well.

I have a podcast with a 10-20 million RMB annual revenue. If I engage in that project and quit other company operations, I should live an easy and relaxing life. The leaders of large and medium-sized enterprises are all extremely hardworking, which is why I say I've never seen a happy entrepreneur.

At the same time, the start-up owners can live a cosy life because they only need to provide salaries to a few employees. An optimal business size is when the boss invites his employees to dinner, and everyone fills a table of 12 seats.

Bessie

Our company has exactly 12 people.

. . .

Wu Xiaobo

Perfect. I once had a conversation with a friend who was the Consul General of Japan in Shanghai about a podcast programme I was running.

He said he also participated in a talk show on Radio Tokyo and asked me how much I would earn from participating in the programme. I told him that was not relevant. We only charge our audience a subscription fee of 180 RMB per season, and we have over 100,000 subscribers. He was shocked by how we operate.

Bessie

The number is simply beyond his ability to imagine.

Wu Xiaobo

Some business models may not work at 10,000 users but will work at 50,000 users. This type of business model can expand its user group by taking advantage of a large population base. When their business exceeds the break-even point, additional user growth does not add much, making the average cost very low.

Bessie

I think Chinese consumers are more willing to try and accept new things. Any new concept in the market will have consumers willing to try it, and of course, they will complain if the product is not good.

Wu Xiaobo

The Chinese market is younger & thus more curious about making and buying new products and services than Europe and the US. This is true both for consumers and entrepreneurs.

Entrepreneurs in the US are also young, of course, especially in the NYC and San Francisco areas. But Chinese entrepreneurs are probably ten years younger than their US counterparts and 20-30 years younger than their European and Japanese counterparts. So China is a vibrant, young start-up country.

Bessie

China has been well ahead in the digitalisation process compared to other countries. Do you think digital transformation is the key to success for SMEs?

Wu Xiaobo

Yes, it's essential. I don't think IQ is why the new generation is performing better than the older generation. It's the tools we use that are constantly evolving.

When I was a journalist 30 years ago, everyone was writing with pen and on paper. I spent 10,000 RMB on a computer in 1993 with my own money.

My colleague did not understand why I need to spend such a fortune on a computer. But he quickly understood the necessity of using a computer because I could write significantly faster than him.

By 1996, we already had the Internet, and it greatly improved our efficiency. It was literally the advancement of tools that made the laggards obsolete. Things change quickly; one generation can become obsolete simply because they don't speak English. Even in today's companies, employees who learn to use advanced office software often outperform those who fail to do so.

The younger generation is usually more curious and willing to adapt to new technologies and tools. People have become obsolete because they don't use new tools. The advent of the Internet has accelerated this process.

We can divide the Internet into two parts, the consumer internet and the industrial internet. The users of the consumer internet will also become obsolete because they refuse to accept new things.

I have an interesting case to share. There is a fruit store near my home, and the owner hands out free strawberries to every customer who follows his enterprise WeChat account. By doing so, he channelled users to his private domain. In the past year, many roadside stores have closed down due to the COVID-19 situation. When I met him a few days ago, I asked him how business was going.

(With humour) He said it was good and then started trying to sell me his subscription service!

The fruits he was promoting come from a company in Xinjiang. We all know that Xinjiang produces the best quality fruits, but it is so far making transporting fresh fruits very challenging.

So this company implemented a subscription service for members to deliver them fresh fruits from Xinjiang monthly. They have been developing channels across the country, especially roadside fruit store owners, and this year they began to work with a few large companies making some exclusive products. If this fruit store owner can accumulate 50-100 regulars like me, he will have a stable business. If he can develop 50 subscription members, that should give him 500,000 RMB of extra revenue.

Suppose he gets a 20% commission, which would be a 100,000 RMB profit. And the reason he can get this extra income is that he has put effort into building his private domain last year.

The key to success for any business is to make good products and sell them. But for SMEs and start-ups, this is harder and requires two skills which usually come with size and experience. Producing quality products requires training artisans, while selling products requires communication skills. A lot of failed start-ups don't master these abilities.

Bessie

Is using web-based tools proof of successful digital transformation for a company? Or do they need to make changes in all aspects?

Wu Xiaobo

The digital transformation of large companies is very intricate. For example, a company that makes shirts and sportswear has many areas that need digitising, but their financial systems, IT and office software are the areas that need it the most.

The most energy-consuming thing for garment business owners is managing inventory. There will always be returned goods in the fashion business. Live streaming has the same problem. In practice, clothing is the type of product that causes the most returns in live-streaming e-commerce, about 50% of returns. Therefore, they need to have a rapid feedback mechanism at the front end.

Order assembly time is a key indicator in the apparel

industry. Many companies can cut this time down to 10 days to speed up their reaction to market trends. And they will need IT systems to help them achieve such goals. From the data, they can better understand their sales status and make rapid order deliveries.

Digital solutions can also be deployed at the store level. Then we can predict product sale cycles and adjust production schedules accordingly through data analysis, which would require flexible production arrangements. Distribution of products is also an important part. A logistics centre can save labour costs through digitalisation by bringing in robots. A robotic hand can rapidly grab the specified items from the corresponding location.

Again, all this would not be possible without the support of a digital logistics system. After large companies complete their digital transformation of various departments such as the financial system, office system, store management system, production line management and logistics centre, they will need a data centre to integrate all the subsystems. This process will take about 4-5 years, and those who move quickly are more likely to prevail. The digital transformation of large enterprises requires significant monetary investment and poses a great challenge to all employees in adapting to new technologies and environments.

Bessie

For large enterprises, a comprehensive digital transformation would take a long time and a lot of resources. But once they completed building their back end and middle platform, the scale effect of large companies will kick in and quickly show some effect. For small companies, will their digital transformation make a big difference?

Wu Xiaobo

There will still be a big difference. Take my company with only ten employees. For example, digitising can help us cut down costs, such as utilising paperless office software to reduce printing or using collaborative office software in internal discussions so that everyone can add in real-time feedback and edit files together. All these can significantly improve our efficiency. And the good thing about China's market is that there are many free solutions available.

Bessie

Many of these tech providers are also SMEs. How do they survive if all their products are offered for free?

Wu Xiaobo

Well, we can take a look at the Xiaoyuzhou podcast app platform. They provide a lot of free content, and now they are making money already.

Bessie

Are you suggesting making money from advertisers rather than users?

Wu Xiaobo

I've invested in a platform called Xiaoetong (a digital tool provider that integrates brand marketing, knowledge product delivery, user management and business monetising), and many people and companies operating live-streaming are using it. We provide a free version with basic functions and a premium version that charges a 2000RMB monthly subscription. And our customers can pay an additional 3000RMB annual fee to get data reports if needed. The more users a platform has, the more likely they are to find a reliable profit model.

Bessie

Maximising users with free service first and then offering customised services that generate profit, right?

Wu Xiaobo

That's correct. Most collaborative office software developers will provide free versions for small businesses. Start-ups today are very different from our predecessors. China used to be a planned economy where business development was based on expansion, with new labour coming into the city. A hardworking entrepreneur with courage will most likely succeed. There are many successful examples from our father's generation.

However, the success of business ventures nowadays relies on luck a lot. Of course, entrepreneurs always have to be diligent and courageous. After all, they have to confront the market uncertainty and make successful innovations.

Bessie

Based on your study of business over the years, large companies are facing more resistance and taking longer in their digital transformations. Does that mean SMEs will have an easier time digitising than large enterprises?

Wu Xiaobo

No, it won't be easy too. Because large enterprises experience less pressure during economic cycles than SMEs, they can cope with such problems by laying off staff. As long as they don't have a systematic financial problem, it's not a major concern.

The latest Evergrande (one of China's largest property developers) issues are its own systemic problems. It is not that they lost the ability to build houses. Instead, their financial system collapsed due to a capital chain rupture. Although SMEs do not have such crisis, they are less resilient to risks.

The Chinese economy has a cycle every four to five years, in two forms: economic overheating and economic recession.

During an economic overheating, SMEs grew rapidly and formed a bubble, followed by massive collapses as the economy turned cold. The latest recession from last year should be the most challenging time for SMEs in the past 20 years.

Companies must provide consumers value with their products, which are reflected in two aspects. First, the company must produce a good product that differs itself from similar products in the market. Secondly, companies need to reduce the cost of obtaining consumers.

The difference between internet products and traditional goods is that we constantly find ways to reduce the cost of acquiring customers and increase re-purchase rates. To reach such a goal, we must make better products and improve consumer relations. Not only the boss but also employees should participate in this process. How can we improve? Can we increase efficiency, reduce costs, and cultivate a better customer relationship?

As long as we keep improving in these aspects through our joint efforts, the business is sure to succeed.

China has the best supply chain in the world. So long as we use all these tools wisely. We can spend less money and achieve better marketing results.

There's a start-up called Ramen Talk. The average age of its four female founders is 26.

Instant noodles were first invented by the Japanese, and this industry is extremely hard to enter. Although there are many instant noodle brands in mainland China, you'll probably struggle if you want to start a new one now. Yet, these four ladies have succeeded. Their success depends on their excellent product quality.

Bessie

Their brand also focuses on health.

Wu Xiaobo

Yes, that's another feature of their products. There are many condiment packs in a bag of instant noodles. If you go directly to an OEM factory and order 2,000 units, they will definitely say no because your order quantity is too little.

Therefore, they rely on a platform like 1688 to assemble their supply chain. Through online marketing on content platforms like RED, they find their initial consumers and steadily build up a brand reputation with excellent product quality. And ultimately made a success of their internet start-up venture.

Bessie

Shein (a Chinese online fast-fashion retailer) uses the same concept, right? They have many SKUs, but each SKU has a small production quantity, which means that their suppliers are willing to manufacture orders for them in small quantities.

Wu Xiaobo

Shein's annual revenue is over 30 billion RMB. They don't have their own factories. They work with more than 3,000 manufacturers. These suppliers are very flexible with production scheduling for Shein. Some factories can even make a pair of customised socks for their customers, which is incredible.

The flexibility of the industrial internet in China these days has given SMEs a great opportunity to establish businesses. There are many industrial internet middle platform companies in China. Some time ago, I visited an industrial internet-focused company under the Sany Heavy Industries group in Guangdong. They did a very interesting project. Fruit farmers use a fruit drying machine to make dried fruit from their strawberry, banana and orange harvests. Such fruit dryers cost 40,000-50,000 RMB each, which is not cheap for them. And there are many fruit dryer manufacturers in Shunde, Guangdong. They are having a hard time selling their machines because very few farmers are willing to spend so much money on fruit dryers.

So this company equipped their fruit dryer with sensors and internet access, enabling them to operate the equipment remotely. For farmers, it is complicated to operate the fruit drying machine, as different fruits require different humidity and drying procedures. This problem is solved when professionals can remotely control the equipment.

As for the manufacturers, the remote-control system enables them to get first-hand local production data. Also, it allows them to rent the equipment instead of selling, and they don't have to worry about losing their investment because they have total control over the equipment. This leasing model allows them to expand rapidly.

Through thousands of fruit drying machines, they could obtain real-time farm product supply information for fruits like strawberries and mushrooms. They also help thousands of farmers by reducing production equipment spending. A 40,000 RMB equipment investment can be reduced to a 2,000 RMB monthly rental fee.

The information collected by the equipment can be consolidated and sold to upstream food firms. With such information, companies can directly connect with farmers and buy their goods, solving the sales problem for farmers. In this way, a small fruit dryer manufacturer has managed to integrate itself into the supply chain and grow into a medium-sized company through digital transformation.

That is the magic of digitisation, through which companies can grow and become bigger. Another scenario is that an SME does not grow in size, but its productivity increases because of digitalisation. The income of a farmer may increase from 20000 RMB to 35000 RMB as a result.

Digitalisation is a process of creating connections. Just as the consumer internet connects single cell phones and computers to form the Internet. The goal of the industrial internet is to connect every machine. There are 6 million looms in China, and still increasing by one million per year. 1.5 million of them are already connected to the Internet.

China produces 25% of the world's garments. When all six million looms in China are connected to the Internet, we will have a real-time overview of the production of jeans, shirts and other kinds of garments. We can find out which regions are producing 50 RMB shirts and which are producing 150 RMB shirts. It also allows us to know which region has spare capacity and allocate orders to it.

By the way, all the excavators in China are online this year, and an excavator index was created.

Bessie

What does this index do?

Wu Xiaobo

The main excavator manufacturers in China are Sany, XCMG and LiuGong.

Excavators are expensive, and the contractors buying them can't be sure that all their equipment will have a high utilisation rate. So for a very long time, such equipment was sold on credit and the manufacturers cannot receive full payment beforehand. Sometimes these companies have to send people to snatch back their excavators when contract disputes arise.

By 2008, there were some changes, and excavator manufacturers started to put remote control systems on their equipment so that they could stop the equipment at their end if customers default on payments.

These excavator manufacturers started the earliest exploration of the industrial internet in China. This excavator index is now included in the annual statistics of the National Bureau of Statistics. We can get data such as how many construction sites are working in China in the second quarter of 2021 and how many hours per day they are working. China may develop a loom machine index or a container index in the future.

Bessie

How do SMEs choose between so many digital tools? What kind of tools are essential in their digital transformation?

Wu Xiaobo

What's a boss's favourite thing?

Bessie

(With humour) Money.

Wu Xiaobo

Yes, it seems that we all agree on this.

What the boss values most is tools that can help him save money and generate profits.

Why do almost all apparel companies start their digital transformation with the operational processes of their retail stores? Because most of the owners of large garment companies in China were born in the 50s and are at least 50 years old. They don't know much about the Internet. Therefore, it is very difficult to convince them to spend 20 million RMB on digital transformation.

The biggest problem for this industry is inventory. Let's say that his inventory is 37% and an order assembly time of one month. I could propose that he spend 20 million RMB on digitalisation and eventually reduce the order assembly time to 10 days and reduce their inventory from 37% to 26%. The inventory reduction alone would save him 20 million. Once the boss understands that all the effort is to help him save money, he will invest in digitalisation.

Bessie

This kind of digital transformation can only be achieved in China with our complete and mature infrastructure.

Wu Xiaobo

Yes, we have the best infrastructure in the world.

Among the 2021 top 200 listed SMEs in Asia by Forbes, 64 companies are from the Greater China region. Let's compare the level of digitalisation around the region. Our country has the most mature and complete system because China has invested in this area for years, giving SMEs an excellent market environment for digitalisation.

Bessie

In the preface of your book Lost Games 1, you quoted an article by economist Wei Jie (a senior economic advisor and vice president of the Chinese Society of State-owned Assets Management) in the Southern Weekend on February 21, 1997, which predicted that "it would be an excruciating phase, and I estimated in ten years, only one out of 200 private enterprises would survive." You were a bit dismissive of his pessimistic arguments at that time, but now it seems that his prediction was correct. Looking back, how do you view your judgment 21 years ago, and what are your thoughts?

Wu Xiaobo

Wei Jie made this statement in 1997 when the Asian financial crisis broke out.

Large-scale enterprise collapse and elimination have been happening all the time. When we look at the top 500 private companies announced by the state recently, only two from 2011 remained on the 2021 list.

Most of the top 10 companies on the 2011 list have problems, such as Hainan Airlines, Suning (one of the largest electronics retailers in China) and Evergrande (one of China's largest property developers).

Bessie

Is it because of over-expansion?

Wu Xiaobo

Each of them has their own problems. Suning has a transformation problem. Evergrande was over-leveraging. Hainan Airlines has troubles in its globalisation process.

Bessie

The digital economy is key in the future of the country's 14th Five-Year Plan.

Can Mr. Wei's prediction also be applied here? That is to say, the future of business will struggle to survive without some degree of digitalisation.

Wu Xiaobo

Yes, digital transformation is one thing that all companies, big or small, must do. Resisting this process is the same as a person living in Shanghai who decides never to use WeChat. Good luck, and I hope he can find a way to buy things here.

However, digitalisation does not guarantee success because everyone is doing it. And digital transformation is one of those things that all companies have to do, with no guarantees of success. The sooner, the better.

Bessie

Your company is a medium to large scale company with a few hundred employees.

Wu Xiaobo

Yes, therefore, I have a significant cost burden.

Bessie

What digital tools are particularly useful for your company?

. . .

Wu Xiaobo

I have two companies with a total staff of about 300. Blue Lion, a financial publishing house, was the first company I started after I left Xinhua News Agency in 2003.

That company is very interesting. It has been 18 years since I started in 2003, during which it has always been profitable and has never lost money. And it has always maintained a staff of 60-70.

The secret of its survival had been written on the wall since the first day I founded the company, which was "to focus only on the best business books".

We only publish financial and economic titles, launching about 80 books a year and generating 10-20 million RMB in profits, an excellent company.

Yet if I ask the editor-in-chief to increase our profits to 30 million next year, I don't think he can do it. This company has always been the top three financial book publishers in China. I hope they continue to do so.

My other company is the 890. Since I started the we-media Wu Xiaobo Channel in 2014, this company has progressively developed many paid-for knowledge products. There is no issue with digital transformation in this process because it is the result of the digitalisation of the cultural industry.

I don't know if 890 will still exist in 20 years.

The key lies in whether the digital financial content it produces will continue to iterate and generate value two decades later. Books are different; they are highly tangible items. I think there will still be a market for paper books in 20 years. At least the experience of the past 20 years tells me that no matter how things change, there will always be people who prefer the experience of reading a paper book.

More than 20 years ago, when Lost Games 1 was

published, the price was 23 RMB per copy. Today, it is still a best-seller at 100,000 copies per year, at 58 RMB per copy due to inflation. The Lost Games 1 is about common sense, changes in marketing and how to deal with them.

Bessie

Don't over-leverage your financing.

Wu Xiaobo

Yeah, it's naive not to be greedy, but you can't be too greedy.

Bessie

One of the major goals of China's 14th Five-Year Plan is to achieve common prosperity, and it seems that SMEs will get a lot of advantages in this process. What opportunities do you think may arise in the next five years that SMEs can grasp?

Wu Xiaobo

I don't think there are many opportunities left. Companies shall fail and will fail. And there might be a bigger surge in the collapse of businesses.

Bessie

What's the reason?

. . .

Wu Xiaobo

The market has become more rational, and people are more cautious now about starting a business. A failure of a business is worse than a stock investment failure. 100,000 RMB of stock investment may still leave you 80,000 RMB. A half-million yuan start-up venture will likely leave you nothing.

When all the looms in China, refrigerators, air conditioners, and washing machines in China are connected to the Internet, who will have the greatest opportunity?

Bessie

I guess it would be the big companies.

Wu Xiaobo

The big company's digital capability won't be limited to China. It will extend its influence throughout Southeast Asia, Mexico and so on. In the future, we will probably have the ability to predict the yearly demand for shirts in Mexico and allocate production in advance.

The biggest beneficiaries of digitalisation are the big companies, which will certainly react the fastest. SMEs need to learn to follow the pace of major players.

Bessie

So SMEs must enhance their own capabilities. For example, they must get a good result when the state big data platform evaluates their credit rating.

Secondly, they must integrate themselves into the ecosystem of large enterprises, binding interests with them.

So when big companies make money, you will have a share too.

Wu Xiaobo

We need to move with the times. For SMEs, individual development is closely linked to the prospects of the country, city, and industry.

Try to understand why it's important for the state, society and industry to prosper so you can achieve personal success. And once it's all figured out, you can try to think about the below questions: How to make a good wonton dumpling and sell it? Of the 100 customers that come in today, how many will come back again within 30 days? How can you get more regulars?

Bessie

Or you can try to find out how to get customers to bring in new customers.

Wu Xiaobo

You can always try to sell more to your customers, like two more fried dumplings.

Wu Xiaobo

For SME owners, the key is to use all the resources available. For the sake of ensuring the safety and liquidity of investments, it's understandable not to invest in stocks or property. It is necessary to renew their perception of all new things. If a 2.3% demand deposit rate is too low, try the

T+0 deposit products offered by banks or institutions. The additional interest income generated by 500,000 yuan may help you hire an extra worker. But if bosses don't keep their curiosity, they can't know such things. And such a resource would be wasted.

Bessie

So bosses must take action to understand what kind of solutions are out there. In fact, there is really a lot of information out there, all you need to do is act positively.

———

4
CHINESE LINGERIE MEETS INTERNATIONAL STRATEGY

If chapter three is our most insightful and entertaining, this chapter features one of our most inspiring guests and her equally inspiring brand, Neiwai.

Neiwai is a leader in women's underwear and apparel and its success has been founded on the clear-sightedness, humility and healthy Chinese pragmatism of its founder, Liu Xiaolu.

First and foremost, the episode tells a great story about a visionary Chinese brand and its rise from a standing start to huge success.

That said, what struck us hardest on first reading the transcript, was how fundamentally different Neiwai's approach is to the more typical, more ad-hoc, Chinese approach that we've seen in earlier episodes.

In essence, Liu Xiaolu has taken a very classical strategic and marketing methodology, one which might be taught on any global MBA programme, and applied it in China. In doing, she has rooted the business in a set of values and issues to which she remains passionately and deeply committed.

As we've seen, this is highly unusual in China; in fact this approach is usually flatly rejected as not applicable or effective in a market which, as global visitors are so often reminded by their Chinese colleagues "is just different".

But of course it isn't, or at least not in every way.

In their relatively short history, Chinese advertising and marketing communications have focused almost exclusively on sales promotions, discounting, special offers and similar 'sales-push' techniques. This is still largely true in the e-commerce era, and is something of a foundational creed for dominant e-commerce platforms like T-Mall, Tao Bao and to a lesser extent, JD.com, where the emphasis is on search rankings, special offers and advertising placement in key page positions.

This has been quite damaging for international brands participating in the mistaken belief that these platforms offer easy access to vast established consumer pools.

Shoppers are there in great number alright, but the brands sit within densely crowded categories which don't cater for 'differentiation'. Sales are driven through proprietary marketing tools to which all competitors have equal access, budget permitting. Increased spending on these tools will usually increase sales, but the extra revenues rarely exceed the additional cost. It's an elegant model if you happen to own one of the e-commerce platforms, but has set many a brand owner on the path to failure.

Over the years we've listened to any number of western marketers explaining their embrace of platform marketing tactics on the basis that 'Chinese consumers are just different'; that unlike us, the Chinese are super-street-smart bargain hunters, too cynical and hard-bitten to respond to anything other than price.

But bargain hunting is not unique to China and, when

the only recognised marketing approach has been to offer sales promotions and incentives, it's hardly surprising to find that the Chinese have become extremely good at it.

More recently, the emphasis has switched to endorsement by Key Opinion Leaders (KOL); celebrities, major or minor, who endorse and showcase a brand or product for money. This was a step forward in terms of sophistication and one which the e-commerce platforms have embraced, but it stops far short of classical 'brand differentiation'. While still new and novel, the KOL approach met with plenty of success, but it hasn't taken savvy Chinese consumers long to realise that a paid endorsement isn't necessarily a reliable one.

China's consumer markets are young, consumer marketing techniques in their infancy and all of this is taking place in a digital economy with a completeness and penetration unmatched in the world. And yet, Chinese consumers are people; human nature and psychology are essentially universal.

A classical branded approach ought to be overwhelmingly attractive in China, partly for its sheer novelty. Might a true consumer brand, offering unique benefits and associating itself closely with issues, ideas and needs that are close to Chinese hearts and minds not stand out and do rather well? Chinese consumers haven't been over-exposed to branded communications; in our experience they often respond far more positively than the more jaded shoppers of New York, Paris or London.

Which brings us back to Liu Xiaolu and Neiwai.

It takes courage to go against the received wisdom. And it's courage which entrepreneurs like Ms Liu seem better able to muster than large international corporations, or even the more entrepreneurial western businesses active in

China. Of course courage alone can be a dangerous attribute, but what is particularly illuminating about Neiwai's story, and about the personal qualities of Ms Liu, is the way in which the brand has matched courage with a carefully considered and well executed strategy.

Ms Liu was educated in China, Hong Kong & the US. Her exposure to international markets, classical strategic and business thought combined with her Chinese heritage has to adapt and apply her strategic ideas and share them effectively with Chinese colleagues, partners and consumers.

One tried and true tactic for international businesses of any size in China is to find another such person to help translate their thinking into local execution but be warned, they are in short supply and these days, more likely to be competing, rather than working for you.

The other lesson here for foreign business people with an interest in China is that there are plenty of attractive niche segments, not usually targeted in this way. Equally, the means of targeting them; chiefly a highly interconnected and sophisticated ecosystem of social media, digital channels and e-commerce, are better developed and more sophisticated than perhaps anywhere else.

So what are the insights in this episode most likely to guide a brand owner towards success? We think Neiwai might summarise them as:

- Find a new consumer need or niche which requires more substance in product, service and thinking than is currently available.
- Build your brand around a theme or topic which is integral to the product category, which can fuel storytelling and command real empathy,

more likely through social media storytelling than advertising.
- Maintain absolute clarity and consistency on exactly what the business is trying to do for its consumers, how and why.
- Take exceptional care in choosing a small but profitable range of SKUs and managing inventory levels.
- Get the balance right between your online and offline presence.
- Exercise equal care and caution in the choice of partners, agencies and especially brand ambassadors.

If this sounds like a standard template for success in any brand driven business, we make no apology. Neiwai offers compelling evidence that this approach is universal.

Better yet, it turns out that doing something which nobody else is doing has as much potential for success in China as anywhere, with the result is that niche brands and strategies may be the only businesses for which the hackneyed 'China billions' argument actually stands up to scrutiny.

Throughout this book we devote a good deal of energy to explaining why China actually is vastly different, even alien, to western ways of viewing the world.

This episode reaffirms that for all the cultural differences, China is populated by people; and people, whether in Europe, Africa, the Americas or Asia have fundamentally the same wants, needs and desires.

———

Transcript:
Neiwai: Classical Branding in China
Broadcast on 3 March 2021
Hosts Bessie Lee, Jennie Liu

Guest
Liu Xiaolu
Co-founder (with her husband) of NEIWAI in 2012.

NEIWAI has been a ground-breaking pioneer in the Chinese market for elegant, comfortable lingerie and underwear. Launched online, NEIWAI today has 2.2 million social media followers and distributes both on and offline to more a million repeat customers.

In 2021, Ms Liu was featured in Fortune China's "Future List of China's Most Influential Businesswomen."

In 2020, a lingerie brand known for its sexy designs suddenly declared bankruptcy and shut down its UK operation. Its world-renowned "sexy myth" started falling apart. Besides the direct impact of the COVID pandemic, several factors have contributed to their business closure, including the rise of feminism, Athleisure's influence on lingerie from the fashion industry, the emergence of No Bra Day and a growing number of female consumers seeking to please themselves rather than others by taking off their high heels and underwire bras.

Women's intimate apparel liberation has become an emerging trend in the global market, including China. In this episode of Beiwanglu, we invited Liu Xiaolu, the founder of NEIWAI, a brand focusing on intimate apparel in China.

She will share her thoughts and observations on the consumption habits shifting towards comfort in the lingerie industry and the awakening of female consciousness.

Bessie

Can you tell us more about how you started your brand?

Liu Xiaolu

Compared to many new brands today, we started very early. It's our ninth year already. We have great expectations for what we want to achieve in our tenth year.

I was born in Shanghai, a city that embraces feminism. I grew up with a very early awareness of gender as a female. When I went to college in Hong Kong at the age of 18 and my first job was related to consumer brands. Then after I finished my studies in the US, I joined a consulting firm. And luckily, all the projects I did were related to marketing strategies for female consumer brands. After five years of working in the consulting firm, I began to consider creating my own brand.

From the beginning, I had two goals. First, the brand must be a female consumer brand because I can try it out as a user to understand our products' features better, its strengths and weaknesses.

Second, the brand must have a cultural value, suitable for storytelling with emotional content. That's why I decided to create a lingerie brand, which has a high entry barrier.

I was very lucky to enter this industry as a newcomer with no design or apparel industry background. The factory owner I initially worked with was very supportive after hearing about my vision to start the brand, and Neiwai placed its first 100,000 RMB order with her.

Back then, I was aware of many lingerie brands in New York and Europe with a long history and products that are simple in design but with great attention to detail and choice of fabrics.

In the Chinese domestic market at that time, we couldn't find such a lingerie brand. This inspired me, so I set a benchmark for our products. Our products need to return to the essence of intimate apparel, using high-quality materials, focusing on comfort and details.

Bessie

Eight to nine years ago, the mainstream of women's lingerie was about sexy lace and push-ups, like the lingerie series from Victoria's Secret. A brand like yours advocates the pursuit of spiritual and body freedom, which completely contradicts the mainstream market trend at that time.

Choosing to make such a niche product took a lot of courage. How did you foresee that women's demand for underwear would return to making themselves comfortable in a few years?

Liu Xiaolu

We did see a little bit of such a trend in the US and

Europe. In 2012, Aerie, a brand of American Eagle, started a body-positive campaign using un-retouched photos of real women. It is very much in line with how I look at the female body.

I feel that many women are too harsh on themselves in the pursuit of a perfect body. That leads me to think about what is the essence of intimate apparel? Good lingerie should be comfortable so that ladies are willing to wear it and feel unrestrained.

With this design goal for our products, I believe there must be a demand for them. Because we are a new brand, I did not expect a high growth rate for the company. We only launched a series of eight panties at the beginning, using high-quality fabrics. We also subdivided the panty types because, at that time, we found that Chinese women's understanding of panties was only briefs and boxers. In the overseas market, there are many types of panties to pair with different bras.

Bessie
So you chose to start by making panties.

Liu Xiaolu
Yes, because it was too difficult to produce bras.

Bessie
So when did you start making bras?

Liu Xiaoyu

It was around the end of 2013.

Jennie

Is it difficult to make bras because of the high cost or the difficulty in design? Where exactly is the entry barrier?

Liu Xiaolu

The major challenge in producing bras is that women have different body shapes, and 1000 females may have 1000 different breast shapes. That's why it's hard for one bra to fit all women.

Even today, it still takes us about a year to develop a bra. It takes a very long time to find ladies with various body shapes to try on our bras and give feedback.

Moreover, the production workflow of bra manufacture is very long, and it uses a lot of accessories, which makes the manufacturing process more complicated. That is why the lingerie market is primarily dominated by traditional brands in the past, who have already achieved a certain degree of monopoly.

We haven't seen many new brands in the last decade. Only in the past year or two did new brands start to emerge. Women of the new generation have changed a lot.

Bessie

Speaking of changes, around 2017, bralette started to gain popularity among female consumers around the world. At the same time, an industry phenomenon happened. Sales of sexy-oriented Victoria's Secret started to decline, a 45% drop that year. In the same year in the UK,

Marks & Spencer saw a 40% increase in the sales of bralettes. With your observation of the change in consumer habits, when did you start to feel an increasing preference for comfortable underwear?

Liu Xiaolu

Since 2013, we have been selling comfortable underwear. We had a series called Zero Sense at that time, featuring a relaxed and unrestrictive feeling. We did some market education in 2013. Uniqlo entered this field earlier, and their underwear category was solely bralettes. It was them who did the initial market education of bralette underwear in China. The true prevalence of bralette has to wait until 2016-2017, which is in sync with the changes in the US market.

Our Zero Allergy series, launched in 2016, was Neiwai's best-selling series, and our sales increased five-fold that year. We experienced great growth on Tmall (a Chinese B2C online retail website, spun off from Taobao, operated by the Alibaba Group) within a year with this product. Looking back, 2012 to 2015 was a challenging time for us because most consumers still prefer push-up bras. But we saw an abrupt shift in consumer perception between 2016 and 2017, especially among young females.

We used to think that women would gradually have higher requirements for comfort after having children (around 28 to 30), and when they were younger, they would prefer sexy, pretty bras. But we find young girls nowadays care more about their own comfort more than other people's opinions. Many girls wear sports underwear every day, which are mostly bras with no underwire. The boom in sports fitness has done a great deal to promote the bralette.

Jennie

Some people say that 2011 to 2017 were the lost years for the traditional lingerie industry. With the advancement of e-commerce, social media and consumer awareness, many new consumer brands, including Neiwai, enjoyed rapid growth in those six years. Based on your observation, what was the trend of the Chinese market at that time?

Liu Xiaolu

Indeed 2016-2018 was the fastest-growing period for Neiwai's online sales. There were very few brands making bralettes at that time, and we were one of the very few brands in the market focused on bralettes. Since our goal was to produce intimate apparel that makes ladies feel comfortable and free, we must not use underwires, which would cause restraint and discomfort.

Such a style can sometimes mislead people into thinking that we were a brand focusing on making underwear for the small-breasted. We achieved many technical innovations at that time, including enhancing support under the bra without using underwires and utilising new insert pads design instead of the traditional cups.

As a result, our products fit well even for ladies with small breasts. Between 2016 and 2018, we achieved four to five folds of sales growth each year, causing many new brands to recognise the huge potential in the bralette underwear market.

. . .

Bessie

The Financial Times had an article last July about the liberation of women's underwear. They combined athlete and leisure to form the new word Athleisure. The article discussed how sports underwear was becoming the latest fashion trend. Sports underwear was only worn by ladies as sportswear initially, but sports underwear is much more comfortable than an underwire bra.

So more and more young women, especially the millennials, are choosing lingerie that can show off their fit and healthy bodies instead of trying to please men or gain their attention. As millennials grow accustomed to wearing sports underwear daily, they have also begun to ditch their high heels. Therefore, both domestically and abroad, in department stores, sneakers now occupy an even larger area in the shoe section and even overtake high heels.

Millennials are more interested in their comfort and pursuing a healthy and fit body. It seems the trending of sports underwear has indirectly contributed to the popularity of the bralette, right?

Liu Xiaolu

Yes, Neiwai has positioned itself as a brand of intimate apparel. We have three major product categories: underwear, loungewear and sportswear. Our sports underwear series started in 2018. At that time, we found many women would go straight to work out after their work day. So we came up with a series of underwear to meet this demand, which is comfortable to wear during the day and suitable for sports. This is a big trend. Young women are trying to meet traditional expectations like being elegant and at the same time, also becoming more neutral or even genderless.

. . .

Bessie

Once I have tried comfortable underwear, I feel l I can't adapt to the discomfort associated with the underwire bra anymore. Our male audience could perhaps try to put on an underwire bra to feel the discomfort of being restrained for hours that many ladies have suffered every day!

Comfortable underwear is a great liberation for women. The millennial generation holds very different values, and bralettes as a banner of women's liberation is very iconic, and this is a trend I am excited to see.

Liu Xiaolu

Yes, once I tried it, there was no going back. This is an entirely irreversible trend, just like the progression of women today. Once women have gained freedom, they will not follow any restrictions that are traditionally labelled for women, such as women should do the right thing at the right age, like getting married and having children.

Young ladies nowadays have more diverse choices. A free mind and body mean they have more choices, choices unaffected by value judgements. The progression of lingerie reflects the female social status progress. We still have a lot of work to do, and our brand will grow along with this new generation of females.

Bessie

One of your advertisements last year used 'NO BODY IS NOBODY' as a slogan. In the past, people usually chose models with great shapes or even supermodels for lingerie ads, but you chose six ordinary women for the campaign.

Liu Xiaolu

This ad created a strong resonance among users online and won several awards last year. Our team came up with the idea. In the past, we thought our products were meant to be shown by models with perfect bodies. Over the past two years, we have developed different lingerie products for women with larger breasts or bodies. Our products are becoming more diversified to accommodate the concept that our body shapes are very different.

We hope that customers of all ages, regardless of whether they have large or small breasts, thin or big, can find the right lingerie for them at Neiwai. Our slogan "NO BODY IS NOBODY" emphasises the body's true form, and we hope to show the comfort and true freedom of mind and body for women. After deciding this would be the theme of our 2020 campaign, we started recruiting female volunteers.

Bessie

I have noticed that among the six female models, there was a senior lady. How did you convince her to do a lingerie commercial?

Liu Xiaolu

Before we started recruiting models in July 2019, we conducted some discussions on social media on what are women's concerns and anxieties about their shape and body.

Based on the discussion, we settled on a few areas getting fat, having breasts too big or too small, pregnancy, childbirth, ageing and scarring.

We received over 70 submissions from women once we began the recruitment process. We waited until the last minute to finalise our selection because we wanted to make sure we could form a natural collaborative atmosphere.

One of our models is already 58. She used to be an actress when she was young, and she is still in great shape. She could dance comfortably in lingerie in front of the camera. Her audition video clearly showed her love for her body, and I think she is gorgeous and should be a role model for all young women.

Bessie

She reminds me of Elon Musk's mother, who is incredibly active in her 70s.

Speaking of advertising, how did you convince Faye Wong (singer-songwriter and actress, often referred to as the "Diva of Asia") to become your global brand ambassador?

Liu Xiaolu

In 2018 we had our first brand advocate, Du Juan (an actress and model). The collaboration worked out remarkably well. She delivered our brand image very well, and we wanted to share some new concepts with our consumers through her. We have pondered for a long time, who would be the ultimate brand ambassador for Neiwai? Through group discussion, we believe it should be Faye Wong. However, the collaboration came to be through a series of coincidences.

At that time, director Maizi (a female dancer, actress and director) was shooting a series of commercials for us with Tan Yuanyuan (a Chinese ballet dancer and principal dancer of the San Francisco Ballet). During a chat with her, she mentioned Faye Wong was also a user of our products.

This led to a smooth communication with Faye Wong's agency team. We felt that Faye was cautious in her choice of endorsement partners, especially with lingerie brands. The core reason for the collaboration to eventually happen was that Faye Wong used and approved our products.

This is the best thing that happened to us in 2020. Of course, our team did all the preparation, including spending lots of time researching Faye Wong's past movies and interviews to determine the project's direction, and we finally pulled off this collaboration.

Jennie

We observe that many new lingerie consumer brands have generally chosen younger female celebrities as brand ambassadors in recent years. And Neiwai has a unique approach compared to them.

Liu Xiaolu

Our style is highly associated with our brand positioning and target consumers. Compared to other brands that use young celebrities as brand ambassadors, Neiwai's target consumers are the new middle-class females. A brand ambassador too young would not be that appealing to them. A young celebrity brand ambassador may be able to bring traffic and short-term sales growth.

But choosing a global brand ambassador should be a prudent decision. The brand ambassador's identity, personality, and experience should match the brand's values and vision. Women like Du Juan, Faye Wong, Tan Yuanyuan and Mai Zi are examples of many new middle-class females. Especially Faye Wong, despite her full life experience, still remains true to her own life choices.

Bessie

I noticed that you have a new product designed specifically for period use called Pantie PRO, a pad-free period panty. Does it really work?

Liu Xiaolu

The key to this product is the use of a new material in the crotch area, with excellent liquid absorption and permeation properties. This product took us about a year to develop. Thinx in the US also has a similar product, but we put more R&D into the material and achieved a better result.

This product release has caused a huge buzz. But from the later review, we found promoting such a new product still needs quite a bit of market education because there has never been such an alternative to feminine hygiene products in China. Still, it has many practical scenarios. For example, using this panty will be much more comfortable when you are unsure if your period is coming or ending. You can also combine it with sanitary products during the period. It's very eco-friendly.

. . .

Bessie

That means you can wear this underwear the whole day when you have a low flow.

Liu Xiaolu

Yes, you do not have to change it during the day.

Bessie

A whole day?

Liu Xiaolu

Yes, it's a hassle to have to change during the day. You can if you want to. If the flow is low, it won't be a big problem to last the whole day. According to statistics, about 33% of women in China suffer from urinary incontinence after childbirth, especially when sneezing, running and exercising. These panties could be helpful to avoid such anxiety.

Bessie

Most of our audience are young women and men. They may not have any sense of how relevant urinary incontinence is. For some women, a natural delivery during childbirth may weaken the muscles needed for bladder control. Sneezing, coughing, running, or even walking fast can cause unintentional passing of urine. That's why the sanitary pad section in the mall also sells pads for urinary incontinence.

Liu Xiaolu

We were surprised that this problem was so common in China, approximately 30%. I didn't know this before, so I had to ask my friend's mother. As it's a rather embarrassing issue, so many people affected prefer not to talk about it.

Through this product, we hope we can make people address these problems more openly. What are the benefits of such a business model for the brand? Following the liberation of women's upper bodies, this product is another very important product to liberate women's lower bodies. The only issue now is that washing the panty is still a hassle, but for people with such demands, it's already hard to stop using it.

Bessie

I want to make a suggestion. There are still a lot of young girls in China who come from families with limited income, and the cost of sanitary pads is still a financial burden for them. Some countries, like New Zealand and Scotland, provide free sanitary pads to teenage girls. I think your Pantie Pro underwear can help this group of people when Neiwai starts to think about doing some charity projects.

Liu Xiaolu

I am also very concerned about this topic. Women spend a

lot of money on their period every month. When we developed Pantie PRO, we wanted to keep the cost down as much as possible. It is not cheap at more than one hundred RMB each, mainly because of the high material cost. We have already done a few charity activities for girls in rural areas, primarily in the form of free bras. That is an excellent suggestion, and our future charity projects will consider increasing support for them in this area!

Bessie

With your current product line focusing on lingerie and loungewear, how will you expand into other areas in the future?

Liu Xiaolu

We have introduced some clothing that is suitable for both home and work. This product category is already one of our core products. In the next year or two, you'll see more Athleisure styles of sportswear.

Jennie

In a previous interview, you mentioned that Neiwai took some insight from Uniqlo's business experience by following the approach of "less SKU and higher inventory". In other words, fewer types of items, but the MOQ (minimum order quantity) for each product is one million. What are the benefits of such a business model for the brand?

Liu Xiaolu

At that time, we only had an online business, which was

well suited for such a model. Uniqlo's model can largely reduce inventory pressure and further reduce the cost. Consumers can get a more affordable price. We thought it was a great model at the time.

But today, we have many physical stores, which require a fair amount of product presentation. And that's the difference between online stores and physical stores. Still, we try to minimise SKU when we design products, and we want each product to match the needs of a certain occasion or a certain group of people, not just to look good or be stylish.

Jennie

I found that Neiwai has the most physical stores among all the popular new consumer lingerie brands. At the same time, traditional lingerie brands that rely on franchising still have a large market share in some lower-tier markets. Will you consider opening more stores or using other means to capture this part of the market?

Liu Xiaolu

We started our business as an online store, and in 2017 we made an important decision that Neiwai must have our own physical stores. For intimate apparel, whether it's lingerie, sportswear or loungewear, customers always want to have the opportunity to try it on and feel the fabric in person. We have more than 100 stores in 26 cities in China today. As we consider intimate apparel a necessity, accessibility for consumers is an important factor.

Bessie

For most underwear, customers must go to a physical store to try it on. The salesperson will also help you make various adjustments. On the other hand, comfortable lingerie doesn't have as many different sizes, reducing fitting needs. Why do you still need so many physical stores?

Liu Xiaolu

The essence of our products is the patterns and fabrics. Therefore, we want our customers to go to our physical stores to experience our products personally. It's not just about fitting but also how your body feels. It is impossible to feel the fabric over the internet. 80% to 90% of the entire Chinese intimate apparel market sales are from physical stores. Some online brands have grown rapidly in sales in recent years, but they still need physical stores to support their market development.

Bessie

How do you choose the locations for your stores?

Liu Xiaolu

Our logic is top-down. We first open stores in the largest shopping mall in big cities, and then gradually expand to other areas. Our stores are mainly located in first-tier cities and provincial capitals of second-tier cities, and this year we will slowly expand to some core second-tier cities. As we have many online users from third and fourth-tier cities, we also hope they can buy our products more easily in the future.

5
FINDING SUCCESS AS A FOREIGN BRAND IN CHINA

Our focus thus far has been fairly high level. We've explored the Chinese market, its home-grown approaches to innovation, product development and strategy, and we've examined all these through the lens of Chinese culture.

This episode is different. On one hand, it has a more practical and operational focus, on the other it's the only episode in this edition featuring a successful foreign owned brand in China.

We've commented already on how relatively rare it is to find a thriving foreign business in China. The success of Myk + (a Danish cleaning & care brand aimed at Mothers with young children) offers valuable insights into how it can be done.

Our guest Yaping has home advantage in terms of her market experience and cultural affinity with Chinese consumers. She also has an insider's knowledge of China's complex, sophisticated social, digital and e-commerce infrastructure.

This is all valuable of course, yet we believe that the

most important factor in Myk+'s success has to do with the category it's in and the very fact of its foreign-ness.

In the early years of China's economic boom, trust and quality concerns led many people to favour international brands. Things have moved on now, and home-grown products are often championed today in a well justified display of national pride. Nevertheless, Chinese shoppers still have positive attitudes towards products from certain foreign countries and associate them with quite strong, if rather stereotypical, characteristics.

It won't startle western readers to hear that in China, France is seen as a world leader in wine and cuisine, Germany for its technical proficiency and reliability, Korea for beauty products and pop culture, Britain for elaborate tradition & etiquette, Italy for its iconic fashion industry and the Nordic countries for their ethical and natural design-driven ethos.

So far, so cliched, but of course marketers in the West have long played up to these stereotypes. In a market like China, where international brands simply weren't available until relatively recently, they offer an especially valuable 'hook', allowing consumers to engage, explore and even gain face by displaying their international outlook.

We've seen already how a brand can redefine its positioning at will when it launches here, but if it also plays to established preconceptions, its prospects are greatly enhanced.

What kind of international brands have an immediate and stand-out advantage in China? The most obvious are brands like myk+, operating in categories which rely heavily on trust. Infant products may be the best example of this but others like optical goods, or health supplements are also attractive.

What's more, in this arena, branding and marketing need not be especially highly polished or sophisticated. Myk +'s approach, despite the over-enthusiastic, slightly ponderous use of marketing buzzwords, has actually been fairly generic.

It is hardly a niche proposition to target mothers who are concerned about the wellbeing and safety of their infant children, nor is it a breakthrough to partner with Key Opinion Leaders (still widely viewed as the only way to market a new brand in China).

In this and similar cases, the key to success is to find a brand with the right provenance and a powerful theme of special interest to a particular group.

Regardless of location, a theme like child care will always tend to have a proliferation of active social media communities. In China, these groups are engaged to an unprecedented degree.

Why?

Partly the immense 'connectedness' of the Chinese' (just under 1.1 billion smartphones users at time of writing; source Statista). Partly the symbiosis between China's modern consumer economy and the new technologies which arrived at about the same time and on which much of its growth is built. Partly also, there's the fact that so many Chinese parents are first-timers (often still only-timers). It may also be difficult to trust publicly available information, so that the Chinese tendency to rely on advice and input from within their family & social network is emphasised.

Myk + was quite right in identifying that trust and safety are an easy and plausible fit with Denmark's reputation for ethical practice. Equally, they understood that

Chinese mothers with young Children are highly amenable to interacting through social media to share their anxieties, experience and recommendations. Most of all, they saw that they had quite a story to tell and one which was guaranteed to hold their Chinese consumers' attention.

One of the most useful, aspects of this episode is the discussion around things that didn't work as well as hoped. Yaping's comments on KOLs for example are informative and led her to a renewed emphasis on the importance of content in social commerce. It's both interesting and suggestive to compare this with other content approaches like that of Bao Dao Optical in the first chapter.

Editor's note: For a briefing on KOL marketing in China, follow this link, courtesy of Daxue Consulting, or scan the QR code below:

Some might feel that Myk +'s story, as told here is a slightly sexed-up, occasionally self-contradictory account of a fairly mundane approach. We wouldn't agree; Yaping's openness in acknowledging the shifts in focus as Myk+ grew is admirable. She, in common with all the guests featured in these chapters, exemplifies the Chinese ability to find the practical and effective path.

Reflecting on this, and all the cases covered in this book, it may be that the Chinese are better at achieving success than explaining how they do it.

I doubt that they would object to our saying so either. More likely, they would shrug and reply that to talk and never arrive is like 'climbing a tree to catch a fish' (缘木求鱼), that is to say, pointless.

It's this irresistible practicality of mindset that shines through these dialogues and, we believe, goes a long way towards explaining the Chinese genius for entrepreneurialism.

Transcript:

Myk + Practical lessons in China market entry

Broadcast on October 19, 2020
Hosts Jennie & Bessie

Guest

Chen Yaping

Ms Chen has over thirty years of experience in brand marketing, advertising, media, and e-commerce operations, first at Mindshare China (part of WPP Group PLC) and more recently as marketing director for Myk +, an ethical Danish mother and baby care brand. Ms Chen was responsible for MYK +'s China market launch and subsequent China and subsequent growth.

Large FMCG brands have substantial marketing budgets and work with many agencies. But small brands that are newly established or just entered China, traditional marketing is not always an option due to the challenges of budget limitations, and a lack of consumer and branding specialisms.

More and more small overseas brands are entering China, including niche celebrity brands, organic home cleaning and care products, nutritional supplements, and health products.

These brands need to be innovative in their marketing, co-operation with key opinion leaders (KOLs) and live-streaming e-commerce strategy.

In this episode, we have invited a marketing director with over 20 years of experience working in China to share her story and some thoughts on how a niche overseas brand can enter the China market and survive.

Jennie

Hello everyone, welcome to join us on this episode of Beiwanglu. I'm Jennie Liu, and I will be hosting with Bessie Lee today.

Bessie

Hello Jennie, hello everyone.

Jennie

We have talked about a lot of trends and observations in the previous programmes. In this episode, we will talk about methodology.

I believe we have many entrepreneurs in our audience. For big brands, they have a relatively rigorous and mature way of operating. The logic is not quite the same for those who want to build new brands from scratch in China or create a small and beautiful brand with a limited marketing budget. Many small brands doing well overseas may encounter some common problems in China's market.

Our guest today, Yaping, has a lot to say on this topic. She has worked in a 4A agency for over 20 years, and she has worked with brands including but not limited to health care products, financial insurance, beverages, food, and automobiles.

Yaping left the agency and became a marketing director of an overseas brand that recently entered China. Her main job was to develop their China market and use social content for brand building and sales promotion. We welcome Yaping to introduce herself and her career, and can you talk about the brand too?

Yaping

Hello everyone. As Jennie mentioned, I have been working in a 4A agency, or rather, a media agency for 20 years. I left the agency in 2017. I joined myk+ as marketing director in the first quarter of 2019.

myk+ is imported from Denmark. The brand was established with the vision that a mother wants the best cleaning and care products for her children.

It's the reason why the founder of myk+ decided to work with a Danish factory to produce their products. The brand's China presence was made possible by China's rising consumption and the Chinese mother's dedicated focus on her children.

Therefore, we believe the timing is good for such a brand to enter the China market now and we had a lot of market insights and perspectives to share. I am delighted to share with you today, from the perspective of a small brand, how we view our operations in China.

Jennie

In the FMCG category, what's the difference between the small brand and the big brand? And how is the current market for their cleaning and care products? Can you share with us some consumer insights on their choice of products, especially with mothers?

Yaping

It's fascinating for me to see how the Chinese market has evolved in the past two years. Big established brands, which have reached a certain economic scale, will use consumer insights to a certain degree, understand the market size, and know how much they should invest, especially the really big FMCG brands like P&G and Unilever.

So for small overseas brands like us, we don't view China's 1.4 billion people market as a whole. Instead, we see the potential niche markets that might evolve from it, along with the social and economic development in China.

It's pretty interesting that our household cleaning and care products are placed together with beauty products and cosmetics in the Tmall system. The category we are in is called Beauty & Personal care. To place myk+ in the FMCG category is interesting because our products are not as fast moving as most people think they are.

· · ·

Bessie

I know there is a story behind the myk+ brand, not just an ordinary household cleaning and care brand. There is a story about the founder and her child.

Yaping

Yes, the founder's child had severe skin allergies and she found that all the household cleaning products and even baby care products in China use many chemical additives.

So it's very hard for her to create a safe environment for her child.

She tried very hard to find products that can help to lower the possibility of triggering her child's allergies. In the end, she found a factory in Denmark called Nopa, the largest producer of household cleaning products in Denmark. When she met with Nopa people and talked about co-operation, she discovered that there is a production line in the factory that makes products without artificial scents, additives or preservatives.

That's how the myk+ brand was established.

Even now, most people in China or even in Asia don't think there is a market for this type of product. But this market has been established for a long time in Europe.

Our brand myk+ has a Chinese name 洣洣 (pronounced 'mimi'), meaning mild. Mild enough for everyone to use and to be kind to the environment.

Bessie

When did this brand enter China?

· · ·

Yaping

We entered China in 2017. In the beginning, it was just our brand founder and some friends doing what I would call a market test.

2017 is the year China started the so-called consumption upgrade. Our marketing effort at the beginning was social marketing, by promoting and introducing the brand concept with the help of KOLs (key opinion leaders) on WeChat and Weibo. We also sell products on our WeChat store. There was no Tmall flagship store in 2017.

Bessie

So, in the beginning, you developed the brand foundation with social e-commerce.

Yaping

We started our operations on WeChat, using the family and friend community approach, and focusing on the brand features. It is designed for children with allergies, made in the Nordic country, pollution-free, with no artificial flavouring and additives. So, telling the brand story in the name of a mother's love for her children is a natural choice.

Jennie

So, the users in the community know each other and share their experiences, make recommendations in the WeChat group, and then purchase products from your WeChat store, right? Instead of using the cross-border e-commerce on the Tmall International platform.

. . .

Yaping

I think it's related to the development of the entire e-commerce industry.

Tmall International became relatively mature during the end of 2017 and the beginning of 2018. Tmall cross-border e-commerce also started during that time. In the beginning, we were more like a purchasing agent. But we didn't go down on this route and gradually began expanding our private domain traffic (a marketing method in which communication with customers is funnelled into private pools on platforms that allow brands to have full control without costs of third-party platforms: Daxue Consulting).

Jennie

I feel that baby products are ideal items to be sold in community groups. I met a French organic food brand person who is planning to enter the China market. He is also considering starting with community building.

It seems like a common practice for baby products brand entering a new market. If it's for women and children, it's easy to make money. And what is the reason?

Bessie

Before the second-child policy was implemented, most women in China only have one child. So this child is very precious to them. When it comes to a product recommended by friends, her confidence in the product is dependent on her trust in that friend.

. . .

Yaping

From the beginning, we have concentrated our marketing and brand promotion effort on mothers. Chinese mothers are a special group of people who value word-of-mouth most.

From the perspective of a traditional marketer, the so-called social sharing, social and KOL marketing are all word-of-mouth marketing from years ago. When we started our marketing campaign in March last year, we worked with many KOLs and active members of many communities, who are mostly mothers. These Chinese mothers are fun and very anxious about their children.

The mother and baby product is a mature market, which looks very profitable, but it has a high entry bar. This is a distinguishing feature of China's mother and baby market.

As a new brand just entering the market, we started by telling a story of a mother's love for her children. And then, we did a lot of product designs, from role selection and brand positioning, all through a process of discussion and testing.

Bessie

As myk+ is a relatively small and new niche brand, you started with a WeChat micro business and built a user community, laid the foundation carefully, and checked the market response before opening the flagship store on Tmall. When all things went well, you continued expanding to other major platforms.

Am I correct?

. . .

Yaping

Yes.

We have constructed and expanded our online and offline operations, including high-end supermarkets, Tmall flagship store, Tmall supermarket, and Jingdong B2C. By July last year, our sales channels covered most online e-commerce platforms and offline high-end supermarkets. And we can carry out brand promotional activities both online and offline.

Jennie

At the beginning of last year, you started seeking co-operation with KOLs. As a brand with little market momentum, no brand and product stories yet, and no consumer insights, what were your main concerns in choosing KOLs? What were your criteria in choosing KOLs?

Yaping

I have to admit that in my 20 years in a media agency using traditional marketing methodology to emphasise the breadth of influence, it was really all about how many fans you have and how much exposure you get. From the beginning of last year, the marketing operations are primarily about brand awareness building.

We knew that we needed mothers to help tell our brand story. To do that, we found many baby-product KOLs. Some of them are ranked among the top five in their category. And the major factor of the ranking is the number of fans. So before May last year, we worked with this group of top KOLs, hoping they could help us build our brand recognition among these particular consumers.

· · ·

Bessie

Did these top KOLs meet your expectations?

Yaping

With KOLs in general, it depends on what your expectations are. As a new brand, it's natural to think we should find some top KOLs to help us promote our brand and products. But on the other hand, just telling our customers our brand story is not enough to make them buy. So, to this extent, KOLs are creating an endorsement for us.

And when we approached the first group of KOLs, our challenge was that they had never heard of us. The potential risk to their reputation if anything were to go wrong meant instant rejection in many cases!

But after the first few successful co-operations things became much smoother. Other KOLs from baby and mother communities began to feel more confident in collaborating with us.

So our first KOL partners were hard to sign-up, but they did open the door to co-operation with others. But to answer your question Bessie, when it comes to gaining social community influence no, they didn't really meet our expectations and we found it very difficult to make sales conversions from their fans too.

Bessie

I guess it's difficult to quantify the effect of endorsement. Having approval from top KOLs makes the collaboration with other KOLs easier.

· · ·

Yaping

Yes, it's difficult to quantify. The obvious benefit is that it becomes easier for us to open new sales channels. For example, when we talk with some KOLs and trying to sell our products on their platform, they usually show no interest in the collaboration.

Because we were unknown, to them and to the market, they had to do more preparation in order to sell our product.

From their perspective, there were easier brands to represent and sell.

They would often ask, "what's the advantage and benefit of selling your product"? Of course, the more we were able to share examples of other successful KOL collaborations, they began to feel that our brand had potential in the China market and become more interested.

From a sales point of view, we achieved more benefits on B2B rather than B2C from this kind of collaboration. It's not an intense co-operation, but it helped us to develop sales channels and promote our brand.

Jennie

So if you decide later to take the B2C approach by working with KOLs and generating sales directly from consumers, what would you have to do differently?

Yaping

After this phase, we started seeing a better sales conversion rate when we co-operated with some popular KOCs (key opinion consumers). Their fan number is not our primary concern. Instead, it's their interaction with fans that we prize. A really good KOL is someone that answers fan's questions, and actively engaged in the community conversations.

In the beginning, we paid more attention to the number of fans and brand exposure generated by KOLs. Later, we valued community interaction and stickiness between the KOL and fans more highly.

Our brand had limited resources. We knew we couldn't copy a big brand's "cast-a-wide-net" approach so right from the start, we knew that e-commerce would be our most import channel.

Once we'd decided this, our sole focus was to find KOLs who could help us with content marketing. We already have a general idea about the campaign, after working with the KOLs. However, the campaign content felt very similar. Maybe it's because we were working with professionals. They were familiar with this kind of collaboration and knew how to introduce our products. As a result, we found most of the content in the first phase very similar. Sometimes I even have a sense of déjà vu. Have I read this article somewhere before?

After the June 18 shopping festival, when we are reviewing our past campaigns, something felt wrong. I feared we have lost the essence of content marketing.

After the first phase, we started to focus on quality content delivery and trying to understand the nature of KOLs and the meaning of content marketing.

Bessie

How did you evaluate the stickiness and interaction

between KOLs and their fans at this stage? Do you have any special analysis tools? Or just simply open the KOL's page and check the interaction between him and his fans?

Yaping

We did two things. We used a mar-tech provider to help us get more data. When you are new to a market and uncertain who the right target is, your competitors can show you the right direction; you can check who they are hiring, for example. Last year, we looked for a partner to provide such data to help us better understand the market.

Having a KOL partner does not equate to running social content marketing. There is still work to be done.

By June, we had a mar-tech technology company to provide us the essential data so we could take a broader perspective on KOL marketing. They helped us identify the right KOL partners and also gave us the latest information on our competitors and their marketing content. From that point on, we had to do things the hard way. When choosing KOLs, we have to check their community interaction, fan stickiness, past articles, group buy histories, and feedback.

Bessie

So there are no tools to help you analyse. It's all about hard work.

Yaping

Yes, at least I don't know of any tools that can meet our needs. After examining the list of potential KOLs, we found they can be divided into three types of people. Parents who like to share baby photos, parents who like to share parenting tips, and parents who like to share product reviews.

All three types are called mother and baby bloggers. If we choose them based on data like the number of fans, article clicks, or social media interactions, the most direct outcome may result in no traffic coming to our store. On the other hand, if we used the right KOL, traffic can be seen immediately from the sales record.

Bessie

Have you ever encountered this scenario? You work with a top KOL, and the community's feedback is mostly positive, some customers even say they have placed an order. But in actual fact, there are no sales.

Yaping

Luckily, we haven't. To avoid a situation like that, it's necessary to have some sales targets in the KOL agreement.

Initially, when we chose KOLs, we hoped they would bring us exposure which could be converted to sales. But we found the result very difficult to quantify.

Later, we found it worked better for content cooperation (but not for group buying) if we avoided setting hard sales goals for our KOLs. We have other means to evaluate the efficiency of our collaborations. We can simply check our sales data. Without sales pressure, our KOLs have no motive to cheat.

Editor's note: For more on group buying, see Nikkei Asia's article, 'The Shakeout in China's Community

Group-Buying Market' (link & url: https://asia.nikkei. com/Spotlight/Caixin/In-depth-The-shakeout-in- China-s-community-group-buying-market).

Jennie

Yaping said mother and baby KOLs could be categorised as sharing life, reviewing products, and group buying. Who can generate a higher conversion rate?

Yaping

It depends on the product type. A product reviewing KOL might be good for baby food products. For products like baby laundry detergent and other environment-related items, sharing life KOLs might be more effective.

I think it depends on the brand and product features. And how you'd like the story to be told. These KOLs deliver their content differently. And their fans also have different purchasing preferences.

It's rare to see one mother and baby KOL falling into all three categories. So you have to ask yourself what you want from the KOLs and choose them accordingly.

Bessie

I want to ask your opinion on Wu Xiaobo's one failed live-stream e-commerce campaign.

Editor's note: Wu Xiaobo, featured in chapter three, is one of China's best and most influential financial writers and publishers.

According to your analysis, popularity correlates to the number of fans. But it doesn't equal to conversion rate. And I don't quite understand why Wu Xiaobo, a top KOL, chose to sell infant milk formula.

Yaping

We can assume a dairy brand approached him seeking a collaboration. He will have reviewed the product and its specifications and confirmed that it's a good and trustworthy one. That's a rational judgment, but it's odd for someone with his particular public profile to be promoting infant milk formula, let alone convincing customers to trust the product and buy.

I don't understand why Wu Xiaobo's business team decided to accept this deal. And why would a dairy company think collaborating with Wu Xiaobo was a good idea? It doesn't make sense.

Jennie

I have the same question too. Why Wu Xiaobo?

Is it also common for mother and baby brands to cooperate with young male stars? I know some cosmetics or skincare brands are doing this. Girls are willing to pay for products recommended by young male celebrities they like.

I found the same dairy brand also hired young male celebrities for their live streaming sales campaign. Why would a mother and baby brand hire someone good-looking but too young to be a dad for their advertising? Do they believe that popularity can bring them traffic?

. . .

Yaping

I think it's all about getting attention.

We can simply treat them as brand advocates. Most young parents grow up in the 90s. So using a celebrity that they are familiar with could help get their attention on the products. From the brand's point of view, their primary motive is to capture the attention of their customers, not to sell products.

Bessie

So it's all about building brand awareness and letting consumers see the products first even if they never heard of the brand before.

They may want to know more about it because their idol endorses it.

In this case, the conversion rate may not be an important KPI for the brand that co-operates with young male celebrities. Instead, KOL's popularity, number of fans, and number of live stream viewers are more important.

We all want to sell, so conversion rates aren't irrelevant. But this kind of brand is about consumer loyalty, trust and connection – conversion metrics are just not the right mindset.

Jennie

What do you think of the fact that Wu Xiaobo only sold 15 cans of infant milk formula on his live-streaming platform?

Yaping

There is definitely something wrong. First, only a tiny proportion of the viewers are mothers. In the group of people watching Wu Xiaobo's live streaming, how many are women, and how many mothers are there? And how many of them believe Wu Xiaobo isn't doing this just for money, and that he had actually tried the product to make sure it's good for their babies. Did Wu Xiaobo make people more interested in the product and be willing to pay for it?

Jennie

Have you ever tried live-streaming commerce? As a small and new brand, will you consider working with KOLs and run some live streaming e-commerce? What is your criteria for choosing such KOLs?

Yaping

We are still trying to find more opportunities to work with Viya and Austin. (Austin Li is China's top beauty influencer; Viya Huang was the queen of China's multi-billion ecosystem of live online shopping until Dec 2021 when she was fined massively for tax evasion and her Taobao live-streaming e-commerce platform suspended.)

Because they have a good fan base, and customers will not feel strange seeing our brand and products on their live-streaming platforms.

These KOLs will choose the products for their live-streaming platforms, and the key factor is that the products must be easy to sell as most of their incomes are from commission. They have to evaluate which products suit their selling profile best. A best-selling product should be well known and cheap, has clear features that can be explained quickly, has high market demand, and has little or no after-sales problems. To be chosen as a "Viya's selected product", a product needs to meet all or most of these criteria.

Bessie

I read a report recently. It says 'Viya's selected products' has a high return rate despite its good sales record....

Yaping

Both Viya and Austin are in the same situation. The problem could be rooted in the nature of their flash sale, the so-called impulse consumption.

The hosts can cloud your judgment too. When they keep yelling, ' there is no stock left, so hurry up' and you place the order without thinking. In fact, a large proportion of the products they sell are fast-moving consumer goods. It's hard to say if you truly need it. Most people place the order first and then decide if they like to pay later.

There are two situations here. One is that you don't pay after placing the order, and the other is that you begin to ask yourself if you truly need it after paying the bill. I don't think the hosts with high return rates create the problem intentionally. It might be just the sheer number of consumers they have. Some of them who ended up buying things would later decide not to keep them. As a consumer, when I need a particular product, I would sometimes order from different brands and then return the ones I don't like later.

. . .

Bessie

It's a common practice for some live-streaming hosts to use click farms. Do you know what proportion of the returns is from click farming? Any KOLs that you worked with used click farming? Or did you find signs of them using click farming services?

Yaping

We have not encountered such a thing. When we worked with Austin last year, our products had a return rate of 20%. It's pretty much within our expectations.

For all the other live streaming we have done on Weibo or Taobao, we haven't encountered any abnormal return rate. I believe click farming happens because many KOLs ask us if they need to meet some KPIs.

Once they have to meet some hard target, they may resort to some measures. I guess it's a common practice in the industry.

Bessie

Take the case with Austin as an example. After all the costs you have to pay, is it still profitable from the perspective of your brand?

Yaping

We break even.

Bessie

But it could benefit your future promotion by using ' an

Austin endorsed product' label on your products. Is that why you chose him?

Yaping

They gave us six months of authorisation to use Austin's name in our product description. And it's pretty handy.

Jennie

I see many products on Taobao that have the Austin tag. So you can also use these words in the name of the product, right?

Yaping

We can't use it on our Taobao product link name, but it's okay to use on RED (one of China's most popular social shopping platforms). For example, when I have a KOL writing content on RED for us, they can say Austin recommends it.

Bessie

How effective is this six-month recommendation by Austin?

Yaping

As a new brand, we need to use all the resources we have.

We have used Austin's selection, Dingxiang mama's

selection, and Niangao mama's selection. They are also KOLs that we have collaborations with. All these efforts are to help us speed up our product sales. Judging from the feedback of our dealers, it's clear that they feel our products are well accepted in the market.

Bessie

You only have six months of authorisation to use Austin in your promotion content. In terms of sales, what's the difference between these six months and after? Besides the fact, it might be easier to open new channels.

Yaping

We didn't have the luxury to look at this matter systematically from the beginning. I must admit it, in the whole process of our brand development, we don't have the time to check the outcome after six months and then decide the next step. We are just putting in our best effort and moving on. We worked with Austin and other KOLs simultaneously and received an accumulated marketing result.

We only knew we were in the right direction. There was no way to quantify how many sales were generated from the collaboration with Austin. We only knew that he helped us sell 3000 pieces in one live streaming event, but there was no way to quantify the after-effects. As a new brand, having an influential KOL to back us up was very beneficial. It's also a good selling point in our marketing content.

Bessie

You know there is a book called The Tipping Point (by

Malcom Gladwell). And I have been watching this KOL live commerce phenomenon. It seems all brands, regardless of their size, are trying very hard to enter the live-streaming rooms of these super influential KOLs like Austin or Viya. All hoping that they can help them create a tipping point for their brand.

Sometimes, with the help of these top KOLs, they can reach their marketing goal in one and a half years. Otherwise, it might take three years using traditional marketing.

Yaping

It does not matter whether you're working with KOLs like Austin, Viya, or taking the brand advocate route. Creating a tipping point is not that easy anymore. Because the China market is highly fragmented.

With new headlines every day, a man-made "big day" is difficult to achieve as planned these days.

Austin and Viya might be able to generate the initial topic, and you are also prepared for the next step. But there are always things happening that you are not ready for.

Under this kind of situation, as a brand director, I will not put all eggs in one basket. Hoping that one KOL can bring huge changes in a short time is not realistic. We distribute our resources to different channels according to their potential and our expectation. I'm no longer sure if the tipping point now was the same as the tipping point five years ago or even a year ago.

Bessie

When you were working in a media agency, the more money your clients spend, the greater the popularity and reputation you can buy for them. You will expect more resources from clients to do more campaigns.

And now you are working for this small brand with few resources, especially at the beginning. It should be very different from what you did before.

Yaping

For me, it's painful to move forward. But I think I'm also lucky. Back then, we can spend money regardless of the consequences but the last three years as a media planner, I felt something was wrong. One of my clients had a problem. All our media data was good or exceeding targets, but the sales remain stagnant.

We were trying to figure out the problem. We also did an awareness check every month, and they ranked first every time. Its brand exposure was excellent. Judging from its share of voice, they still ranked first. All the data showed their brand was competitive. None of us knew what happened. It seemed the agency had done their job well, but the sales didn't match all the effort.

Bessie

So, did you figure out what had happened before you left?

Yaping

No.

Bessie

What did you learn in that last year at the agency?

Yaping

As a media-planner, my role was to meet my KPIs and to serve my clients well. In general, I should maximise the commercial delivery. We have done all the things promised and even carefully scheduled the efficiency of the delivery. Back then, we calculated the effectiveness factors in digital terms.

To some extent, I think the division of work may be too fine, both for us and the client. And there is no one watching the case holistically. My client and I were so frustrated at that time. They appreciated my dedication and devotion. We believed as long as we followed the procedures, conduct case review and analysis, we could figure out what could be done right in the next step. No, we didn't find a solution. It seemed no one knew what to do and no one dared to say what to do next.

I guess you have a very different mentality now. Is it because you are representing the brand directly? Or is it because you do things differently now?

Yaping

The first difference is that we go from large-scale operation to micromanagement, like checking how KOL interact with fans. Of course, that's our own choice to do things to that detailed level because we planned our operations around social marketing.

The second difference is that we can monitor the outcome in almost real-time. The effect is very obvious. It's not something that we can't grasp anymore.

When I was still in a media agency, we were already very realistic. We had to worry about media channels and distribution rate, preparing follow-up campaigns according to breakthrough rate.

A creative agency usually doesn't need to consider distribution and other things. Good media content is all they need to worry about. That's why in the later phase of the campaign, our clients will feel that the media agency is on their side, caring about their business much more than the creative agency.

And now, when I operate the campaign myself, I can see the effect right away. Not because I do more things than before, but I have the ability to check our traffic simply from the flagship store data and can tell if we have a good KOL or a bad one.

Bessie

In other words, when you find the outcome deviates from your expectation, you can quickly trace back to find out what went wrong.

Yaping

Yes, that's the difference between now and then. I think my time as a media planner trained me well. When choosing KOLs, I knew exactly what their tasks should be. So I can make sure that my purpose and the means to achieve it are correlated. I think this is the best gift from my working experience as a media planner.

With this experience, I am fully aware of the situation. For example, if I want to know how much traffic is generated by a specified KOL, I can just check how many coupons were claimed by customers and how many are used. I can even tell how much a customer has spent on our product page from the Tmall analysis tool. All these data can help us review if our KOL has a reasonable task. If not, we can adjust it for the next day instead of having to wait till the next month, by communicating with the live stream team.

It's totally different from what we did in the media agency. Here, we have to react fast.

Jennie

When a small brand is running its own campaign, they can be very efficient and adjust quickly. What's the most significant role of media agencies when they operate a campaign for a brand?

Yaping

When I was in a media agency, their most important task was coordinating different platforms and simultaneously running operations in the main channels. We do more strategic thinking and see the bigger picture.

Considering the media environment and business model at the time, campaigns could be done this way and produce good outcomes. We don't have that much data or direct involvement of all steps in the process. To a certain degree, we rely on experience to get the general direction.

For the brand I'm operating now, my old experience doesn't always work. Now I spend much more time reading reports than I used to. It doesn't mean all my old experiences are useless because I'm running a small brand. The big challenge for me is knowing which part needs changes according to the current situation.

Twenty years of training in the media agency taught me to react fast to new challenges.

Many of our new practices are very similar to the old school way, like how we recognise the proportion of regular and new customers, how to run a promotion on regular customers and new fans. It's so similar to the loyalty programs from the old days.

Bessie

Before the mid-90s, advertising agencies had many departments, like creative, media, and even PR. They were relatively complete in terms of their functions. From the mid-90s, they became more specialised and segmented. Media agencies started to show up. In short, they significantly scaled up the content delivery. Companies specialising in PR, event organisation, and online or offline business started to show up. This trend started from the mid-90s.

Like what Yaping said earlier, at that time, the media environment or its vendor is relatively simple. Specialised departments still operated on the same or a small range of vendors. But after years of specialisation, many specialist agencies have turned territorial. And now they need to worry about their financial report, profit and loss, and team engagement.

Many young professionals nowadays never served in a full-service advertising company. They began their careers as PR managers, media or creative managers. Everyone is highly specialised now, and their companies are becoming more and more focused on their own self interests.

In this era, Yaping mentioned both media and the end user's time are fragmented. Who is the person struggling most in this situation? I guess that would be the brand. And the bigger they are, the more daunting the marketing responsibility it becomes. Some of our clients might need to deal with 20-30 agencies at the same time. Each of these agencies has their own agendas and ideas.

Of course, you can simply designate one as the leader to run the operation and hope they will co-operate seamlessly, which never happens. So the brand client has to do most of the heavy lifting.

That's the situation Yaping encountered in her last year as a media planner. Every agency has to meet the KPI, and make sure the data looks good or even exceeding the goal. But it doesn't translate to the sales results. They are disconnected. And no agency can deliver a complete analysis, step by step, to show their client why there is such an outcome. Because they only see their own part.

That's why some big advertising agencies are creating project management groups for their important clients by integrating all the functions into a single entity, back to the 1980-1990 agency model. On the other hand, Yaping's small brand is capable of end-to-end tracing and managing all the information. Any situation could be traced back very quickly and adjusted accordingly.

I think the industry needs to change, but restructuring all the agencies and deciding who will take the lead are still big topics yet to be answered. So back to the agency turf war, we mentioned before. In this digital era, the digital agencies will naturally think they are leaders to integrate others. But how can a top creative agency allow themselves to be integrated into a digital agency that's smaller and less famous? Some collective wisdom from the bosses may be the key to meet the challenges of the digital era.

. . .

Yaping

I think that's why many clients are back to the so-called in-house agency model. Since none of the agencies can take the responsibility, they have to do it themselves.

The most painful transition for the traditional agencies is that they lack the project management capability in the digital era. It includes not just media but also content creation, consumer data management, and content delivery.

When I was still in the traditional agency, we didn't have the concept of project management and also lack the ability to do so. Only between 2008-2010, some media agencies started creating their digital team and digital project management.

So I think this is a process of integration and talent upgrade. Today, the marketing department of a brand does things like managing media content, choosing KOLs, and organising fans, which used to be the job of an integrated agency. And I found their abilities are better than the agencies' to a certain extent.

Bessie

If there is a chance for you to return to an agency, will you consider it?

For those talented people in the agency who feel stuck and don't know how to make a transition, what's your advice for them?

Yaping

I have asked myself this question. And I don't have a clear yes or no answer. If an agency boss comes to me and asks for my help, to make some changes in his company, I think I'm qualified.

After 20 years of experience in the agency, I am very familiar with their system. I would return with some conditions. If I am returning just as an office head, I will think the scale is too small and I would decline.

Only when they want to make some fundamental changes on how the company works. I will probably return if there are ambition and courage in the offer. I have always felt that the agencies know all their problems. They just lack the determination and courage to change.

When I was working for an international 4A company, I have a lot of resources. The truth is that it is tough to introduce new things there, let alone make any changes or introduce a new concept to customers.

The more customers know, the more work for us. I often feel sorry for our clients. Their agencies do not introduce new thinking and new technology. It's a kind of fear if you know too much and you would find out that I am actually not that competent at all.

I think the situation in the 4A agencies is that they always tend to do the safe thing. And in many cases, the clients cannot even pinpoint the weaknesses of their agencies. When I contact my former colleagues, they seem busy but not under much pressure. The International 4A companies are still well and sound. Maybe they still haven't seen the end of the road yet.

Bessie

For those who want to make a transition, do you think they can do it within the 4A agency, or do they have to leave first?

. . .

Yaping

I think it's possible to do it in the 4A agency. Because their customers already have the requirement and so does the market. In my last two years in the traditional agency, my client gave me a lot of flexibility to try new things.

They told me they understand we are in a fast-changing market. They didn't expect us to know everything. So we are all in this together to figure out the way. For me, it's a trust that carries the responsibility to make it right.

Bessie

So the most important thing is your determination. Simply waiting for other people to help will make the transition very difficult. On the other hand, with determination, one can make the transition, whether from inside or outside the system.

Yaping

Yes, I think it's not limited to 4A agencies. It applies everywhere. You have to be aware of the situation and act accordingly. Working in a 4A agency is not an excuse to stay put. They have inherent advantages to help you make the transition because there are so many resources at their disposal. You don't need to start everything from scratch.

AFTERWORD

The China Hack & Beiwanglu teams thank you for reading this book and hope you've found it informative and entertaining.

We think it gives a good snapshot of Chinese grassroots enterprise in recent times, although it should be noted both that the Chinese business environment moves quickly and that the global pandemic has caused substantial disruption to some of the entrepreneurs interviewed here and their businesses.

Beiwanglu continues to grow its subscriber base quickly and we look forward to bringing you further transcripts and interpretations in future China Inside Out publications.

To listen to the original Chinese language podcast, you can click on any of the links below (kindle edition) or scan the QR codes:

Apple Podcast

Spotify

小宇宙 Xiaoyuzhou

喜马拉雅FM Himalaya FM

AFTERWORD

网易云音乐 NetEase Cloud Music

QQ音乐 QQ Music

Those familiar with WeChat will know that we can't provide a direct link, but you can access the Beiwanglu account on the app by searching for 贝望录+

For further information on the team principals, podcast or

book, please refer to Bessie or Peter's LinkedIn profiles:

Bessie Lee

Peter Bomer

Or write to:
Peter Bomer 马乐天
Founder

The China Hack
Suite 163, 2 Lansdowne Row
Berkeley Square, Mayfair
United Kingdom
W1J 6HL

Printed in Great Britain
by Amazon